DEC 1 2 2019

READY, SET, Dough!

BEGINNER BREADS FOR ALL OCCASIONS

Rebecca Lindamood

AUTHOR OF *NOT YOUR MAMA'S CANNING BOOK*

PAGE STREET
PUBLISHING CO.

D1223822

PAGE STREET
PUBLISHING CO.

Copyright © 2019 Rebecca Lindamood

First published in 2019 by

Page Street Publishing Co.

27 Congress Street, Suite 105

Salem, MA 01970

www.pagestreetpublishing.com

All rights reserved. No part of this book may be reproduced or used, in any form or by any means, electronic or mechanical, without prior permission in writing from the publisher.

Distributed by Macmillan, sales in Canada by The Canadian Manda Group.

23   22   21   20   19   1   2   3   4   5

ISBN-13: 978-1-62414-904-7

ISBN-10: 1-62414-904-9

Library of Congress Control Number: 2019940368

Cover and book design by Rosie Stewart for Page Street Publishing Co.

Photography by Rebecca Lindamood

Printed and bound in the United States

Page Street Publishing protects our planet by donating to nonprofits like The Trustees, which focuses on local land conservation.

This book is dedicated to

my husband, Lindy, and my sons, Liam, Aidan, Ty, Leif, and Rowan.
You guys are my rock and my reason. Thank you for being my guys. As Julia Child
said, "You are the butter to my bread. The breath to my life."

Contents

INTRODUCTION

I have said it more times than I can count, but the only way I cut carbs is with a bread knife. Clearly I am not on the low-carb bandwagon. Because bread is the staff of life, my daily sustenance and the most delicious thing on Earth. Carbs complete me, man.

This is because bread is a powerful thing.

There is very little on Earth that moves me quite as quickly to a deep, abiding feeling of well-being as the scent of bread baking in the oven. The aroma makes me feel comfort, happiness and a sense of contentment. I know I'm not alone in this feeling, too.

Studies have been done showing how the smell of bread affects people. They've demonstrated a link between the sweet smell of baking bread and the likelihood of people to linger longer in grocery stores, be kind to strangers, or make an offer on a home they're walking through for a viewing.

I am grateful to have been born into a family in which my mom, dad and grandma all baked bread, so I have never been worried about whether or not I could make bread. Baking bread is the thing that we did to show love for each other and freshly baked bread was the scent of my youth.

Bread baking is an intimidating endeavor, though, when you didn't grow up around people who happily involved you in the process. It has an air of mystery and magic, this ability to turn simple ingredients such as flour, water, and yeast into a golden brown, nutty-smelling loaf of bread. The truth is, though, that like many things, it's simple when someone breaks it down and walks you through the steps. That is exactly what *Ready, Set, Dough!* is here to do.

I am on a solemn mission to demystify bread and to make the process of making it fun. You don't have to be to the bread-pan born to be well-bread. Bread is *everyone's* birthright, and I can help you make bread that's impressive enough to share with anyone but good enough to keep for yourself and eat warm from the oven.

In these pages, you'll find nine different methods of preparing dough that will yield 74 different bread recipes. In other words, if you just learn these nine simple methods, you'll have a bread-filled cornucopia of possibilities. But I don't leave you hanging with a book full of recipes and no one to hold your hand; I'll walk you through specifics on methods to make your bread turn out perfect every time (hint: you might be measuring incorrectly!), a discussion of what equipment you actually *need* to bake bread, tips on how to freeze and thaw your bread for best results, information about ingredients, and recipes for using up leftover bread if your eating can't keep pace with your baking.

We'll start things off with an entire chapter filled with breads that are done—from start to finish—in just one hour. Mixed up in just one bowl, these recipes are the ideal introduction to bread baking.

Each one of the categories in the book has a fool-proof classic recipe that goes with it, for example, the World's Fastest Sandwich Bread (page 15), Classic Pizza Dough (page 38), Braided Italian Bread (page 58), Toastable English Muffin Bread (page 76) and so much more!

But it doesn't stop there, even though those are incredible breads. You also have Asiago Herb and Garlic Bread (page 20), Pepperoni Soft Pretzels (page 92), Classic Onion Poppy Seed Bialys (page 107), Barbecue Bacon Cheeseburger Stuffed Rolls (page 62), Chocolate-Stuffed Oat Buns (page 132), and Corn Dog Bread (page 144) among many, many other mouth-watering recipes that are easy enough for beginners to make, but tasty and unique enough that experienced bakers will love making them, too.

Please tag @foodiewithfam in photos you post on Instagram of the bread you made because I cannot wait to see the fruits of your baking labors. Happy baking, friends!

Rebecca Lindamood

Bread-Baking 101:
BREAD-BAKING BASICS TO MAKE YOU LOOK LIKE A PRO

You don't need much for your very first loaf of bread: just some flour, salt, water, and yeast at the bare minimum. We'll get into ingredients, but first, let's talk basics about the process and get the "rules" out of the way.

To get started in bread baking, there are a few guidelines to keep in mind.

First and foremost, measure carefully. This is not "the man" keeping you down, it's simply the best way to ensure that your end product will most closely resemble the intended results. When you go to the trouble of baking bread (or cakes or cookies or anything!), you probably have a pretty specific end product in mind. Measuring carefully is the first step in eliminating variables that could mess up your bread.

Here's a little bit of truth you might not have heard before: there's a very good chance that you have been measuring flour incorrectly most of your life and you're not alone. I measured my flour the wrong way for many years until I learned something very important. And that one crucial thing to know is . . .

The very best way to measure your flour for any baking recipe is by weight. That's why you'll find the weight measurements for various flours given in each recipe in this book. One cup of all-purpose flour weighs 4.25 ounces (120 g).

Flour has a tendency to settle and become compacted in bags or containers. Because of this, a cup of flour measured by dunking a measuring cup into a bag and shaking to level could weigh as much as twice that amount. If you follow that to the logical next step, that means you could be putting in twice as much flour as the recipe creator intended, and that will give you a very different end result.

I highly recommend purchasing an inexpensive kitchen scale that allows you to measure pounds and ounces or kilograms and grams. These are available at all big box–type stores, many online retailers, hardware stores, and some better-stocked grocery stores. The scale doesn't have to have a lot of bells and whistles.

If you're morally opposed to having a kitchen scale or your budget doesn't allow it, you can certainly get very close to the accuracy of weight-measured flour by using the following method. Holding your measuring cup level over your flour container, use a spoon dipped into the flour to sprinkle flour over the cup, and repeat until you have a slightly overfull cup. You then either use the handle of the spoon or the straight back edge of a butter knife to level the contents of the cup. You do not want to shake the cup to level it, as that compacts the flour again. I fully acknowledge that this method is a little more time consuming, but measuring flour accurately is the best advice I can give in making bread. You can see why I prefer weights, right?

When measuring other dried ingredients and yeast into the mixing bowl, add them in the order they appear in the recipe in little piles around the edge instead of sprinkled over the center. This is not as crazy as it might sound at first. And technically, it's not necessary, but I find it makes my life much easier given the wild and crazy schedule my family keeps.

Take Asiago Herb and Garlic Bread for example. This recipe includes cheese, yeast, sugar, salt, Italian seasoning, rosemary, crushed red pepper flakes, granulated onion, and granulated garlic. If you're counting, that's nine different dry ingredients you're adding to the flour.

Now imagine you get midway through adding those ingredients to your bowl of carefully measured flour and you get distracted by the doorbell or a phone call from Grandma or having to pick up a sick kid somewhere. If you've made little piles of your cheese, then yeast, then sugar, and so on, you're going to see those three little piles in the flour and know you left off with the sugar, but you still need to add the salt, Italian seasonings, etc. All of a sudden, what sounded like crazy obsessiveness now sounds like a good idea leading to tasty bread!

That's right. Add your yeast right in with the dry ingredients. Back in Grandma's day, active dry yeast needed to be dissolved in warm water with a pinch of sugar to activate it before being mixed into everything else. These days, yeast is formulated and processed differently and can be measured right into the dry ingredients with no harm done to the recipe. My authority on this is none less than the King Arthur Flour company whose bakers are known for their baking expertise. I find eliminating this one step makes it much less of a production to bake a loaf of bread.

When you measure your water or other liquid, use a liquid measuring cup. These are also inexpensive and handy to have around. While it is important to measure your liquids accurately, it's also important to be a little flexible about how much water you add.

So many factors contribute to how much liquid needs to be added to a recipe, including the relative humidity of your kitchen, weather patterns, altitude, age of the flour, and more. What's crazy is the amount of liquid your flour can absorb can change from hour to hour and day to day.

Every time I add liquids to my recipes, I refrain from adding all of it at once. I usually reserve about ¼ cup (60 ml) or so in the measuring cup. There's a method to this madness.

It's impossible to judge and calculate all of the aforementioned contributing factors just by standing in your kitchen, so holding back on a little bit of the water is the best way to avoid having to do the "This dough is too wet, I must add more flour" dance.

After I stir the dry ingredients with the liquids until a shaggy dough forms, I start kneading the dough; whether by stand mixer or by hand. After the dough really comes together, I can tell whether it needs the rest of the water. If the dough is really sturdy or has dry pockets, I add the water about 1 tablespoon (15 ml) at a time until it is smooth and elastic.

Unless otherwise noted in the recipe, most dough should be supple, elastic, and smooth. It is okay for it to be tacky; in fact, that's most often preferable. You want to avoid dough that sticks to you or the bowl or the counter instead of itself. "Tacky like a Post-it note, but not sticky" (source: King Arthur Flour website) should be the benchmark.

Making the most of this water trick is something that comes with a little experience, but the best way to gain that awareness is to really observe how this works by practicing reserving a little bit of the water so you can see the difference it makes.

While we're on the subject of liquids, let's talk temperatures. Particularly in recipes in the One-Hour Breads chapter (page 12), very warm liquids—120 to 130°F (50 to 55°C)—are preferable. We're talking hot-tap-water warm, for reference. If the recipe calls for water, you can use hot tap water or water warmed but not boiled in a kettle, saucepan, or microwave. Likewise, if the liquid in the recipe is milk, it should be warmed to about that temperature with one of those methods.

This temperature encourages activity in the yeast, which makes rising time quicker.

Don't heavily dust your counter with flour. If you've taken the time to carefully measure your flour, don't tinker with the results by throwing flour all over the place. You end up working as much flour into your dough as you put on the counter. The best bet is to just flour your hands, wipe them over the counter, then flour your hands once more before turning the dough out to knead it or shape it. This should be more than enough extra flour without altering the texture of the dough.

If your room is cold, it will take longer for your dough to rise. This is just unavoidable. A cold room slows the activity of the yeast. Warm liquids will help to some extent, but if you're baking in the tundra, your dough is going to take a while to hit that all-important "doubled in bulk" stage. If your room is drafty, this is also going to be a problem as it might both slow the activity of the yeast and dry the surface of your dough. This won't likely render your bread inedible, but it sure won't be as impressive as it could otherwise be.

Don't despair if you have a cold, drafty kitchen, though. I have a few solutions to help offset those effects. First, you can set your dough—in a covered bowl—to rise in your closed oven with the light on. That light should provide enough warmth to gently encourage your dough to rise. If you're still finding it to be too poky for your liking, you can set the oven to warm (about 170°F [77°C]) for just 3 or 4 minutes and then shut it off. You don't want it to come all the way up to temperature, because you'd be starting the cooking process. You just want to add a little warmth to the party to wake up those yeasties.

If for some reason you can't use your oven as an ad hoc proofing box, you can put your covered bowl of dough in an actual cardboard box with a mug full of freshly boiled water set beside it. Close the box and voila! You've created your own perfect climate for budding bread dough.

And last but not least, don't be afraid to find a nice, warm, draft-free spot in your house to designate as the place to let your dough rise. In the winter, I often set my bowls of dough behind the wood stove. It's perfectly cozy, free of jumping kids and pets, and guaranteed to be left alone as long as it needs to be. One word of caution, though: if you put your bowl of dough out of sight, set a timer so you remember to check on it. Ask me how I learned this. Sigh.

Speaking of covering mixing bowls, shower caps work really well! This handy, dandy trick was one I learned from my stepmom, Valerie. She had a collection of shower caps that she kept in a container because they came three for $1 and they stretched to fit most of her mixing bowls. The bonus was that as long as the dough didn't explode in the bowl, they were reusable. If you don't want to shuffle shower caps around in the cabinet, you can definitely use a piece of plastic wrap or a dampened tea towel.

It's not all about the timer: watch and touch the dough to gauge its progress. If it has approximately doubled in size, looks puffy, and holds onto indentations made when it is gently prodded with two fingers, it is likely ready to shape.

If the recipe calls for a briefer, second rise, use the same visual and touch tests to see if it is ready to bake.

When a recipe says to preheat the oven, make sure it reaches the temperature before you put your bread in to bake. Notice I said when. This is because the longest chapter in this book is filled with bread recipes that you must put into a cold oven for them to work.

That said, when a recipe calls for preheating the oven to, say, 375°F (190°C), wait until your oven actually has reached 375°F to put in the bread. Don't hoist the loaves in at 325°F (165°C) and think it's close enough. The temperatures in bread recipes have been tested to give you the best rise, color, texture, and flavor in your finished loaf, so stick with them.

As difficult as it is, don't cut into that hot loaf of bread. Guys. I know firsthand and intimately the torture that is taking a gorgeous loaf of bread out of the oven, smelling that amazing aroma, looking at the shiny crust, and forcing myself to wait to slice into it. But science has my back on this one. Ugh. I shake my fist at you, science.

Stick with me on the breakdown of why this is, then I'll happily give you the exceptions to the rule.

While a loaf of bread is baking, the yeast is in its happy place, all warm and cozy giving off gases. Those gases expand and create bubbles in the gluten structure of the dough you made. This makes the dough rise and gives your dough the soft but chewy texture you love so much.

When you remove a loaf of bread from the oven, it doesn't cool to room temperature instantly. It takes a while to come back down to ambient temperature and to reach equilibrium with the room, even when turned out of the hot pan onto a cooling rack. That's just the law of thermodynamics and principles of heat transfer at work. It's inevitable.

While the bread temperature is equalizing with that of the room, important changes are taking place inside the loaf. The flour is finishing hydrating, in other words, distributing the moisture you added to it. The matrix you created with the gases from the yeast and the flour's gluten is setting and firming up into a solid structure. The moisture at the center of the loaf is migrating outward toward the crust.

And what does all this have to do with your hungry eyes and your bread knife? When you cut or tear into the hot or warm loaf, you're interrupting that slow, measured cool-down and setting of structure. You're short-circuiting the process. Not only are you rapid-cooling it by breaking open the loaf, but you're also compressing the structure with the pressure and sawing action of your knife. You're undoing all the work the yeast did for you.

But here's where autonomy comes into play and I tell you that rules are made to be broken. I am the first person who will tell you enthusiastically that warm bread is magical. So if you're willing to commit to eating that whole loaf warm, I say go for it. Just remember that the bread is going to be much softer and it isn't going to have any staying power. You need to have it consumed within an hour.

Of course, for every rule there's an exception or two. There is no sane person on Earth who would expect you to wait for a pizza to come to room temperature for the crust to set up. And one of the true pleasures in life is eating a bagel fresh from the oven without anything on it whatsoever. The truth is that if you've taken the time to bake yourself a loaf or two of bread, you owe it to yourself to try it warm at least once. And if anyone gives you a hard time, tell them you're conducting a scientific experiment so you can see how bread changes as it cools.

For detailed instructions on shaping round loaves, information on ingredients used in the book, and a discussion of which equipment you need to make the breads in this book, see the Bread Geek chapter (page 177).

Ready? Set? Dough!

Faster Than a Grocery-Store Run:

ONE-HOUR BREADS

Breads made from the World's Fastest Sandwich Bread dough (page 15) are a thing of beauty and wonder. These are by far the easiest breads in the entire book but they make you feel like a bread-baking wizard. With this recipe, you'll learn how to make a gorgeous, crusty, fine-crumbed loaf in one hour, from start to finish. This is a crazy-simple approach to bread baking that has made countless friends and Foodie with Family readers feel like pros.

All of the recipes in this chapter are a great place for a beginning baker to start, but they're also good enough that veteran bakers will come back to them time and again. These breads are as irresistible as they are pretty and simple to make. Each can be made into a free-form round loaf or baked in a bread pan, so they're even more versatile. Because of the incomparable convenience and the deliciousness of the recipes in this chapter, it is the longest chapter in the book.

If you've never baked a loaf of bread before in your life, start with the World's Fastest Sandwich Bread. It's a good name for a great bread, but the name doesn't even begin to cover the life-changing aspects of this bread. Of course it makes a great sandwich bread at incredible speed, but the bread is equally good sliced and toasted with whatever you love best on toast, cut into thick slabs to soak up gravy or soup, and turned into garlic bread to accompany your favorite pasta and salad.

After you try the World's Fastest Sandwich Bread, move along to the Asiago Herb and Garlic Bread (page 20), Papa's Dilly Bread (page 24), Spinach Parmesan Bread (page 19), Pumpernickel Sandwich Bread (page 28), Bacon Cheddar Scallion Bread (page 27), Crazy-Quick Lofty Dinner Rolls (page 32), Mini Bread Bowls for Soups and Stews (page 35), and Harvest Spice Apple Bread (page 31).

It's true that I prefer to make these using a stand mixer for the sake of ease, but you can most certainly pull the dough together by hand with a sturdy spoon and bowl or in a bread machine. I don't advise baking these in a bread machine, though, because you can't add the pan of hot water to the oven, which is crucial to the method.

If you do have a stand mixer or bread machine, you'll simply mix with a spoon in the bowl of your stand mixer until a shaggy dough forms as noted in the recipe, but you'll add the dough hook attachment to your mixer and knead on medium speed for 4 minutes instead of by hand. Cover the bowl with a shower cap, a damp tea towel, or plastic wrap and proceed to rise and shape the loaves as the recipes instruct.

WORLD'S FASTEST SANDWICH BREAD

One hour from start to finish is all you need to make the World's Fastest Sandwich Bread, which is also the go-to sandwich bread around my house. I've had a version of this recipe on my blog for years, and boy do people love it. "I ate this until I was dizzy. It's so good it should be illegal"; "It works—as is—at 3,000 feet above sea level!"; "I have to say to anyone reading this recipe that it actually works. No. Seriously. It actually works." These are some of the real comments from people who love it as much as we do.

You can have this bread done in the same amount of time it would take you to pull a brush through your hair, put on shoes, grab your wallet, run to the store for groceries, and get home. By making this yourself, you'll be rewarded with much tastier bread for the minimal effort it takes.

Yield: 2 loaves

6 cups (1 lb, 9.5 oz [723 g], by weight) all-purpose flour

2 tbsp (24 g) instant or active dry yeast

2 tbsp (25 g) sugar

1 tbsp (18 g) kosher salt (if using table salt, reduce to 1½ tsp [9 g])

2 cups (480 ml) very warm water (about 120°F [50°C])

¼ cup (60 ml) olive oil, divided

Mix the flour, yeast, sugar, salt, water, and 2 tablespoons (30 ml) of the olive oil in a large mixing bowl with a sturdy spoon until a shaggy dough forms, then knead until the dough comes together and becomes smooth, about 4 minutes by hand or machine. Form a smooth dough ball. Return the dough to the bowl, cover with a clean tea towel, and let rise in a warm place for 15 minutes.

Divide the dough in half and form it into two tight dough balls (see page 177) or loaf shapes. You can place the balls or loaves directly on a rimmed baking sheet or in standard-size loaf pans. Gently flatten the dough balls. Drizzle each loaf with 2 tablespoons (30 ml) of olive oil, then use a sharp knife to slash the tops of the loaves about ¼ inch (6 mm) deep.

Place the loaves on the middle rack of a cold oven with a pan of hot tap water on the rack below it. Close the oven, set the heat at 400°F (200°C), and set the timer for 40 minutes. It is imperative that you start this in a cold oven!

After 40 minutes, remove the bread from the oven and transfer to a cooling rack to cool completely before slicing.

LIGHT-SPEED WHOLE WHEAT BREAD

A couple of little ingredient swaps are all that it takes to transform the World's Fastest Sandwich Bread into a whole wheat loaf that very well may become the one you make to have on hand all week. It's a toasty loaf perfect for slicing for sandwiches, toast, and snacking.

Yield: 2 loaves

4 cups (1 lb, 1 oz [482 g], by weight) all-purpose flour, plus extra for dusting

2 cups (9 oz [255 g], by weight) whole wheat flour

2 tbsp (24 g) instant or active dry yeast

2 tbsp (25 g) sugar

1 tbsp (18 g) kosher salt (if using table salt, reduce to 1½ tsp [9 g])

2 cups (480 ml) very warm water (about 120°F [50°C])

¼ cup (60 ml) olive oil

Mix the flours, yeast, sugar, salt, water, and olive oil in a large mixing bowl with a sturdy spoon until a shaggy dough forms, then knead until the dough comes together and becomes smooth, about 4 minutes by hand or machine. Form a smooth dough ball. Return the dough to the bowl, cover with a clean tea towel, and let it rise in a warm place for 15 minutes.

Divide the dough in half and form into two tight dough balls (see page 177) or loaf shapes. You can place the balls or loaves directly on a rimmed baking sheet or in standard-size loaf pans. Press down gently to flatten them, then dust a teaspoon of flour over each loaf, rubbing with your hands to distribute the flour. Slash the tops of the loaves three times.

Place the loaves on the middle rack of a cold oven with a pan of hot tap water on the rack below it. Close the oven, set the heat at 400°F (200°C), and set the timer for 40 minutes. It is imperative that you start this in a cold oven!

After 40 minutes, remove the bread from the oven and transfer to a cooling rack to cool completely before slicing.

SPINACH PARMESAN BREAD

There's a local chain of grocery stores in my part of the country that sells the most tempting loaves of spinach Parmesan bread. These fragrant loaves, glistening with garlic olive oil, have a crumb absolutely packed with flecks of bright green spinach and Parmesan cheese. I cannot think of a single bread that tastes better toasted or dunked in minestrone. Leftovers make world-class croutons that are good enough for snacking by themselves, but are amazing on salads, too.

Yield: 2 loaves

6¼ cups (1 lb, 10.5 oz [750 g], by weight) all-purpose flour

2 cups (160 g) shredded Parmesan cheese, divided

2 tbsp (24 g) instant or active dry yeast

2 tbsp (25 g) sugar

1 tbsp (18 g) kosher salt

1 tbsp (3 g) dried Italian seasoning

1 tsp granulated garlic

2 cups (480 ml) hot tap water

1 lb (454 g) frozen chopped spinach, thawed and squeezed to remove as much liquid as possible

4 tbsp (60 ml) Garlic Olive Oil (page 173) or plain extra virgin olive oil, divided, plus a little for drizzling

Mix the flour, 1½ cups (120 g) of the Parmesan cheese, yeast, sugar, salt, Italian seasoning, garlic, water, and spinach together in a large mixing bowl with a sturdy spoon until a shaggy dough forms, then knead until the dough comes together and becomes smooth, about 4 minutes by hand or machine. Form a smooth dough ball. Drizzle a little oil in the bowl. Return the dough to the bowl, flip to coat with olive oil, cover with a clean tea towel, and let it rise in a warm place for 15 minutes.

Divide the dough in half and form into two tight dough balls (see page 177) or loaf shapes. You can place the balls or loaves directly on a rimmed baking sheet or in standard-size loaf pans. Gently flatten the dough balls. Slash the tops of the loaves three times, drizzle each loaf with 2 tablespoons (30 ml) of olive oil, and sprinkle with the remaining ½ cup (40 g) of Parmesan cheese.

Place the loaves on the middle rack of a cold oven with a pan of hot tap water on the rack below it. Close the oven, set the heat at 400°F (200°C), and set the timer for 40 minutes. It is imperative that you start this in a cold oven!

After 40 minutes, remove the bread from the oven and transfer to a cooling rack to cool completely before slicing.

ASIAGO HERB AND GARLIC BREAD

Asiago cheese, Italian herbs, and garlic turn our everyday one-hour bread into the most gorgeous brown, cheese-crusted and cheese-studded, herbed, garlic bread I've ever had the pleasure of tearing apart with my teeth.

Yield: 2 loaves

6 cups (1 lb, 9.5 oz [723 g], by weight) all-purpose flour

1½ cups plus ⅔ cup (245 g) grated Asiago cheese, divided

2 tbsp (24 g) dry yeast

2 tbsp (25 g) sugar

1 tbsp (18 g) salt

1 tbsp (3 g) dried Italian seasoning

1 tsp each: dried rosemary, crushed red pepper flakes (adjust up or down according to heat preference), granulated garlic, and granulated onion

1 tsp minced fresh garlic (optional)

2 cups (480 ml) hot tap water (120 to 130°F [50 to 55°C])

4 tbsp (60 ml) Garlic Olive Oil (page 173) or extra virgin olive oil, divided, plus a little for drizzling

Mix the flour, 1½ cups (170 g) of Asiago cheese, yeast, sugar, salt, Italian seasoning, rosemary, red pepper flakes, granulated garlic and onion, fresh garlic, and water together in a large mixing bowl with a sturdy spoon until a shaggy dough forms, then knead until the dough comes together and becomes smooth, about 4 minutes by hand or machine. Form a smooth dough ball. Drizzle a little oil in the bowl. Return the dough to the bowl, flip to coat with the olive oil, cover with a clean tea towel, and let rise in a warm place for 15 minutes.

Divide the dough in half and form into two tight dough balls (see page 177) or loaf shapes. You can place the balls or loaves directly on a rimmed baking sheet or in standard-size loaf pans. Gently flatten the dough balls. Slash the tops of the loaves three times and drizzle each loaf with 2 tablespoons (30 ml) of olive oil. Divide and gently pack the remaining ⅔ cup (75 g) of Asiago cheese over the tops of the loaves.

Place on the middle rack of a cold oven with a pan of hot tap water on the rack below it. Close the oven, set the heat at 400°F (200°C), and set the timer for 40 minutes. It is imperative that you start this in a cold oven!

After 40 minutes, remove the bread from the oven and transfer to a cooling rack to cool completely before slicing.

SUPER SPEEDY POTATO BREAD

This extra fluffy version of the World's Fastest Sandwich Bread is so far from ordinary white bread that you may have to rethink white bread entirely. It's full of flavor and lovely to look at, but this loaf really shines when it comes to texture: springy, but tender. This bread is my husband's favorite bread for sandwiches. These incredible loaves bake up huge and are great for sandwiches of any type, but it also makes my favorite base for our Breadcrumb-Crusted Quiche (page 158).

Yield: 2 loaves

5½ cups (1 lb, 5.25 oz [600 g], by weight) all-purpose flour, plus extra for dusting

½ cup (30 g) plain instant mashed potato flakes, any brand

2 tbsp (24 g) instant or active dry yeast

2 tbsp (25 g) sugar

1 tbsp (18 g) kosher salt (if using table salt, reduce to 1½ tsp [9 g])

2 cups (480 ml) very warm milk (about 120°F [50°C])

¼ cup (60 ml) olive oil or melted butter

Mix the flour, potato flakes, yeast, sugar, salt, milk, and olive oil or melted butter together in a large mixing bowl with a sturdy spoon until a shaggy dough forms, then knead until the dough comes together and becomes smooth, about 4 minutes by hand or machine. Form a smooth dough ball. Return the dough to the bowl, cover with a clean tea towel, and let the dough rise in a warm place for 15 minutes.

Divide the dough in half and form into two tight dough balls (see page 177) or loaf shapes and gently flatten. You can place the balls or loaves directly on a rimmed baking sheet or in standard-size loaf pans. Press down gently to flatten, then dust a teaspoon of flour over each loaf, rubbing with your hands to distribute the flour. Slash the tops of the loaves three times.

Place on the middle rack of a cold oven with a pan of hot tap water on the rack below it. Close the oven, set the heat at 400°F (200°C), and set the timer for 40 minutes. It is imperative that you start this in a cold oven!

After 40 minutes, remove the bread from the oven and transfer to a cooling rack to cool completely before slicing.

PAPA'S DILLY BREAD (SPEEDY COTTAGE CHEESE DILL BREAD)

My dad, also known as Papa to the grandkids, makes Dilly Bread every year as a Christmas gift. Everyone looks forward to getting a couple of loaves to slice up and slather with butter or to toast and top with fried eggs. This speedy one-hour version of Papa's bread hits the spot while we wait for Christmas to roll around. Springy, tender, and bursting with dill and onion flavor, these loaves are incredible and are one of my favorites to use for the Mini Bread Bowls (page 35).

Yield: 2 loaves

6½ cups (1 lb, 12.5 oz [808 g], by weight) all-purpose flour, plus more for dusting

1½ cups (315 g) small-curd cottage cheese

2 cups (480 ml) hot tap water

¼ cup (20 g) dehydrated minced onion

2 tbsp (24 g) instant or active dry yeast

2 tbsp (25 g) sugar

1 tbsp (18 g) kosher salt

2 tbsp (6 g) dried dill weed

2 tbsp (3 g) dried parsley

1 tbsp (7 g) dried dill seed (optional)

1 tsp granulated onion

Combine the flour, cottage cheese, water, dehydrated onion, instant yeast, sugar, salt, dill weed, parsley, dill seed (if using), and granulated onion in a large mixing bowl with a spoon until a shaggy dough forms, then knead until the dough comes together and becomes smooth, about 4 minutes by hand or machine. Form a smooth dough ball. Return the dough to the bowl, cover with a clean tea towel, and let the dough rise in a warm place for 15 minutes.

Divide the dough in half and form into two tight dough balls (see page 177) or loaf shapes and gently flatten. Form each half into a ball and place 5 to 6 inches (13 to 15 cm) apart on a baking sheet that has been lined with parchment paper or a Silpat, or has been lightly greased. Gently flatten, dust the top of each loaf with flour, then use a sharp knife to slash the top of the loaf about ¼ inch (6 mm) deep.

Arrange the racks in your cold oven so that one rack is on the very bottom and one is positioned in the center of the oven. Place the baking sheet with the loaves on the center rack and a bread or cake pan that is full of very hot tap water on the bottom rack. Close the oven and set the heat to 400°F (200°C). It is imperative that you start this in a cold oven! Set your timer for 40 minutes.

After 40 minutes, remove the loaves from the oven. The crusts should be a deep brown and quite firm. Transfer the loaves to a rack to cool completely before slicing.

BACON CHEDDAR SCALLION BREAD

I took a loaf of this to share at the ballet studio where my son studies and to say it got a big reaction is putting it mildly. The artistic director, Sergio, asked where he could buy it. A woman's eyes rolled back into her head when she tasted it. Another one stashed a couple of pieces to take home. It's ridiculously delicious, and almost unbelievable that you can make bread *this good* in an hour. But make it you can, and you will often!

Yield: 2 loaves

5½ cups (1 lb, 7.25 oz [660 g], by weight) all-purpose flour

2 cups (264 g) diced cheddar cheese plus ¼ cup (28 g) shredded cheddar cheese

1¼ cups (140 g) chopped or crumbled crispy cooked bacon

1 bunch green onions, thinly sliced

2 tbsp (24 g) instant or active dry yeast

2 tbsp (25 g) sugar

1 tbsp (18 g) kosher salt

1 tsp granulated onion

2 cups (480 ml) body-temperature water

Nonstick cooking spray (optional)

2 tbsp (30 ml) Garlic Olive Oil (page 173) or plain extra virgin olive oil, divided

Mix the flour, diced cheddar cheese, bacon, green onions, yeast, sugar, salt, granulated onion, and water together in a large mixing bowl with a sturdy spoon until a shaggy dough forms, then knead until the dough comes together and becomes smooth, about 4 minutes by hand or machine. Form a smooth dough ball. Return the dough to the bowl, cover with a clean tea towel, and let rise in a warm place for 15 minutes.

Line a rimmed half sheet pan or quarter sheet pan with parchment paper or lightly spritz loaf pans with nonstick cooking spray.

Divide the dough in half and form into two tight dough balls (see page 177) or loaf shapes and gently flatten. Drizzle 1 tablespoon (15 ml) of the olive oil over each loaf. Slash the tops of the loaves three times, then divide the shredded cheese over the top of each loaf, packing gently onto the loaves.

Place the loaves on the middle rack of a cold oven with a pan of hot tap water on the rack below it. Close the oven, set the heat at 400°F (200°C), and set the timer for 40 minutes. It is imperative that you start this in a cold oven!

After 40 minutes, remove the bread from the oven and transfer to a cooling rack to cool completely before slicing.

PUMPERNICKEL SANDWICH BREAD

Deep, dark, molasses-y, and chewy-but-light, this pumpernickel bread has so much character that it just might be your new favorite sandwich bread. You don't want to skip over this one if you're a fan of darker breads. It is lovely fresh, but makes the most memorable and irresistible toast and croutons, too. Top a slice of this, toasted, with a fried egg with a runny yolk, and you'll be in heaven!

Yield: 2 loaves

5½ cups (1 lb, 7.5 oz [666 g], by weight) all-purpose flour

½ cup (65 g) Pumpernickel Bread Base (page 172)

2 tbsp (24 g) instant or active dry yeast

2 tbsp (25 g) sugar

1 tbsp (18 g) kosher salt

1 tbsp (15 ml) olive oil

2 cups (480 ml) hot water

¼ cup (40 g) yellow cornmeal

Nonstick cooking spray (optional)

Mix the flour, Pumpernickel Bread Base, yeast, sugar, salt, olive oil, and water in a large mixing bowl with a sturdy spoon until a shaggy dough forms, then knead until the dough comes together and becomes smooth, about 4 minutes by hand or machine. Form a smooth dough ball. Return the dough to the bowl, cover with a clean tea towel, and let rise in a warm place for 15 minutes.

Divide the dough in half and form into two tight dough balls (see page 177) or loaf shapes and gently flatten. Pour the cornmeal onto a dinner plate and roll the dough in the cornmeal. Take any cornmeal that doesn't stick to the surface of the dough and sprinkle it over a parchment- or Silpat-lined rimmed baking sheet or in standard-size loaf pans lightly spritzed with nonstick cooking spray. Ease the dough onto or into the prepared pans. Slash the tops of the loaves three times.

Place the loaves on the middle rack of a cold oven with a pan of hot tap water on the rack below it. Close the oven, set the heat at 400°F (200°C), and set the timer for 40 minutes. It is imperative that you start this in a cold oven!

After 40 minutes, remove the bread from the oven and transfer to a cooling rack to cool completely before slicing.

HARVEST SPICE APPLE BREAD

This bread skirts the line between being a dessert bread and a savory bread with fruit in it. When asked what he thought about it, my husband described it as being "like raisin bread, but with apples." You'll find tender pieces of apple throughout this autumnal spice bread made with our fragrant Chai Spice Blend (page 173). This is the only one-hour bread that I don't suggest cooking free-form. Cooking this bread in a loaf pan helps this soft dough keep its shape much better as it bakes.

Yield: 2 loaves

3 tbsp (38 g) sugar

2 tsp (5 g) Chai Spice Blend (page 173)

1 apple, peeled, diced into ½-inch (13-mm) pieces

6 cups (1 lb, 9.5 oz [723 g], by weight) all-purpose flour, plus extra for dusting

2 tbsp (24 g) instant or active dry yeast

1 tbsp (18 g) kosher salt

2 cups (480 ml) very warm water

3 tbsp (45 ml) melted butter

Nonstick cooking spray

In a small mixing bowl, use a fork to toss together the sugar and Chai Spice Blend, then toss in the apple cubes. Set aside for 5 minutes while you measure everything else.

Mix the flour, yeast, salt, water, apple mixture, and melted butter together in a large mixing bowl with a sturdy spoon until a shaggy dough forms, then knead until the dough comes together and becomes smooth, about 4 minutes by hand or machine. Form a smooth dough ball. Return the dough to the bowl, cover with a clean tea towel, and let rise in a warm place for 15 minutes.

Lightly spritz two loaf pans with nonstick cooking spray. Turn the dough out onto a clean surface and divide in half. Form each ball into a tight oval and ease into the prepared loaf pans. Gently flatten, dust the top of each loaf with flour, then use a sharp knife to slash the tops of the loaves about ¼ inch (6 mm) deep.

Arrange the racks in your cold oven so that one rack is on the very bottom and one is positioned in the center of the oven. Place the baking sheet with the loaves on the center rack and a bread or cake pan that is full of very hot tap water on the bottom rack. Close the oven and set the heat to 400°F (200°C). It is imperative that you start this in a cold oven! Set a timer for 40 minutes.

After 40 minutes, remove the bread from the oven. The crusts should be a deep brown and quite firm. Transfer the loaves to a rack to cool completely before slicing.

CRAZY-QUICK LOFTY DINNER ROLLS

These dinner rolls just may change your life. They're buttery, mile-high, fluffy, tender-but-chewy, and basically exactly what dinner rolls should be. I admit it makes me feel a little like a magician when I pull a pan of these from the oven just one hour from the time I started mixing together the dough. It's insane, really. Nothing this good should be this fast and easy, and yet these rolls are! Aside from gracing your bread basket at mealtime, these rolls make terrific slider rolls.

Yield: 20 rolls

6 cups (1 lb, 9.5 oz [723 g], by weight) all-purpose flour

2 tbsp (24 g) instant or active dry yeast

2 tbsp (25 g) sugar

1 tbsp (18 g) kosher salt (if using table salt, reduce to 1½ tsp [9 g])

2 cups (480 ml) very warm water (about 120°F [50°C])

½ cup (120 ml) melted butter, divided

Nonstick cooking spray

Mix the flour, yeast, sugar, salt, water, and ¼ cup (60 ml) of the melted butter in a large mixing bowl with a sturdy spoon until a shaggy dough forms, then knead until the dough comes together and becomes smooth, about 4 minutes by hand or machine. Form a smooth dough ball. Return the dough to the bowl, cover with a clean tea towel, and let rise in a warm place for 15 minutes. Lightly spray a 9 x 13-inch (23 x 33-cm) baking pan with nonstick cooking spray.

Divide the dough in twenty equal-size pieces. Roll each piece of dough into a tight ball (see page 177) and arrange in five rows of four each in the prepared pan. Place on the middle rack of a cold oven with a pan of hot tap water below it. Close the oven, set the heat at 400°F (200°C), and set the timer for 35 minutes.

After 35 minutes, remove the bread from the oven and brush generously with the remaining butter. Place the pan on a cooling rack to cool for at least 10 minutes before serving. If you want to slice the rolls for sliders, you'll need to let them cool completely before slicing.

NOTE: You can also use the World's Fastest Sandwich Bread (page 15), Light-Speed Whole Wheat Bread (page 16), and Super Speedy Potato Bread (page 23) to make these rolls. Just prepare the dough as instructed in the other recipes and use the shaping and baking instructions found here.

MINI BREAD BOWLS FOR SOUPS AND STEWS

These Mini Bread Bowls use the very same technique and same dough as any of our one-hour breads. Tiny boule loaves are a natural for hollowing out and filling with chowder or stew. Don't let that confine you, though. It makes any dinner feel special to put individual loaves of bread at each setting, and they're awfully good served as plain old (if you can call it that) bread, sliced, toasted, or dunked into whatever sauces you want to sop up.

Yield: 4 generous mini-loaves

1 batch of the World's Fastest Sandwich Bread (page 15), Light-Speed Whole Wheat Bread (page 16), Spinach Parmesan Bread (page 19), Papa's Dilly Bread (page 24), Bacon Cheddar Scallion Bread (page 27), or Pumpernickel Sandwich Bread (page 28)

2 tsp (7 g) flour, for dusting, divided

After following the instructions for making the dough and letting it rise, turn the dough out onto a clean surface and divide into four equal pieces. Form each into a ball and place 5 to 6 inches (13 to 15 cm) apart on a baking sheet that has been lined with parchment paper or a silicone baking mat, or has been lightly greased. Gently flatten each dough round, dust with a ½ teaspoon of flour, and rub to distribute the flour. Use a sharp knife to slash three lines across the top of the loaf about ¼ inch (6 mm) deep. This allows the steam to escape the baking loaf without the loaf tearing.

Arrange the racks in a cold oven so that one rack is on the very bottom and one is positioned in the center of the oven. Place the baking sheet with the loaves on the center rack and a bread or cake pan that is full of very hot tap water on the bottom rack. Close the oven and turn the heat to 400°F (200°C). Set a timer for 35 minutes. After 35 minutes, remove the loaves from the oven. The crusts should be a deep brown and quite firm. Transfer the loaves to a rack to cool completely before slicing.

To make bread bowls for soup, use a sharp knife to cut a circle about three-quarters of the way deep into the top of the bread loaf, leaving an edge or rim of about ¾ inch (2 cm) all the way around. Use your fingers to pry out the center plug of bread, keeping as much of it intact as possible so you can butter it, toast it, and use it as croutons. Heat the bread bowl in the oven as you toast the croutons. Serve and enjoy!

Ridiculously Good

PIZZA

If you are what you eat, then I am, in large part, pizza.

I argue that it is the perfect food: a complete meal—with bread, flavorful sauce, cheese, and toppings. The sky is always the limit when it comes to pizza, and the possibilities are almost endless.

Everything is literally riding on the crust, though. It is the most crucial part of the pizza, and seems to be the part most people struggle with perfecting. Because there are so many types of pizza, I am including two different styles of pizza dough that should cover almost all of the most popular varieties of pizza pies.

The Classic Pizza Dough (page 38) may not sound like it's going to wow you, but it is. It's a fantastic pizza dough that is equally perfect as a base for the Classic Homestyle Sheet Pan Pizza (page 40), Wood-Fired or Stone-Cooked Pizza (page 43), or Cool-Kitchen Grilled Pizza (page 44). It's simple to work with and holds well in the refrigerator for up to a week.

That's right, you can keep this dough in the refrigerator for a whole week, and up to three months in the freezer. In case I need to make it more clear, that means you can make dough on Saturday and have pizza every night of the week if you feel like it, and I sometimes do.

But perhaps as exciting as how long it keeps is the fact that you can whip this dough into garlic knots or calzones, as well! This dough is just about as perfect as a pizza dough can be.

The Best Pan Pizza Dough (page 39) has legions of fans for some very good reasons. This no-knead dough admittedly needs to be made the day before you intend to use it, but you'll love it so much it'll become a regular on the calendar. It, too, is incredibly simple to make and yields a pizza that is reminiscent of pan pizzas at some of your favorite restaurants: chewy, crisp and deep brown on the bottom and edges, with just the right amount of toppings. It's going to make you look like a professional pizza maker!

And what else can you do with that dough? It makes a killer Detroit-Style Pizza (page 48) that would do the Motor City proud. And prepare yourself to feel like an old-school Italian baker, minus the crazy 4:00 a.m. wake-up time. You can use this very same bread to make crackling-crusted, flour-dusted, roasty, and delicious Bakery-Style Ciabatta Loaves or Rolls (page 54) in your own home.

CLASSIC PIZZA DOUGH

If Classic Homestyle Sheet Pan Pizza (page 40) is your thing, this is the ultimate pizza dough. But that's not all it's good for; it is the ultimate pizza dough for making Italian-style Wood-Fired or Stone-Cooked Pizza (page 43), or making Cool-Kitchen Grilled Pizza (page 44). It yields a chewy crust with large air bubbles. One recipe yields quite a lot of dough, but because it stores well (and actually improves!) in the refrigerator for up to six days and in the freezer for up to three months, it makes sense to make the full batch. Pizza isn't the only place this dough is golden, too. It also makes terrific Better-Than-Pizzeria Garlic Knots (page 53) and "Choose Your Own Adventure" Meat-and-Cheese Calzones (page 50).

Yield: 3 half-sheet-pan–size pizzas, 8 (12-inch [30-cm]) or 10 (10-inch [25-cm]) round pizzas

9⅓ cups (1 kg, by weight) type "00" flour, or 8 cups (1 kg, by weight) all-purpose flour

2 tsp (12 g) kosher salt

2½ tsp (10 g) active dry yeast

2⅔ cups (630 ml) lukewarm water

1 tbsp (15 ml) olive oil, plus extra for the bags if you plan to save dough for later

Whisk together the flour, salt, and yeast in a large mixing bowl or the work bowl of a stand mixer. Pour in the water and olive oil. Stir together with a sturdy spoon until a shaggy dough forms. Knead with floured hands or by stand mixer for 10 minutes on medium or until the dough is smooth, elastic, and stretchy.

Return the dough to the bowl. Cover the bowl with a shower cap, plastic wrap, or a damp tea towel and let it rise in a warm, draft-free place for 1 to 2 hours, or until approximately doubled in size and puffy.

Divide the dough into your desired size. Use your hands to roll each piece of pizza dough into a tight ball and allow it to rise for 20 more minutes before baking. Or, you can store this dough in the refrigerator for up to 6 days or in the freezer for up to 3 months before using. To store the dough, label a zipper-top freezer bag with the size of the pizza. (Use one bag per round of dough you wish to use later.) Drizzle 2 teaspoons of olive oil in each bag, rub around with your hands to make sure the inside is well coated, and insert one dough ball into each prepared bag.

NOTES: To use refrigerated dough, place the dough in its bag on the kitchen counter and allow it to come to room temperature and rise for an hour before you want to use it and bake it.

To use frozen dough, transfer the bag of dough to the refrigerator the day before you plan to use it, then onto the counter to come to room temperature an hour before you wish to bake it.

BEST PAN PIZZA DOUGH

Pizza made from this dough might be the best thing you've ever made in your kitchen. There's no getting around it, you have to plan ahead to make it. The bad news is that it needs to be made at least 10 hours but up to 26 hours before you plan to cook it. But the good news is that it only takes about five minutes to mix it all together; the rest is resting time and it is 100% worth the wait! This is a dough that is designed to spread itself in the pan (more waiting time, but again, worth it!) so with all that time you saved by not kneading and spreading the dough, you can get a real start on your long-neglected reading list or watch a few episodes of your favorite TV show.

Yield: 2 (10- to 12-inch [25- to 30-cm]) "I Can't Believe This Is Homemade" Pan Pizzas (page 47) or 2 (9- to 13-inch [23- to 33-cm]) Detroit-Style Pizzas (page 48) or 3 medium-size ciabatta loaves or 12 ciabatta rolls (page 54).

3 cups plus 1 tbsp (14 oz [397 g], by weight) bread flour (see Notes)

2 tsp (12 g) kosher salt

½ tsp instant yeast

1½ cups (360 ml) water

Nonstick cooking spray

Mix together the flour, salt, yeast, and water until the dough is evenly moist and there are no more pockets of dry ingredients. Spray a large bowl or entrée-size plastic container with nonstick cooking spray. Scrape the dough into the prepared container. Cover the bowl or container tightly with plastic wrap and let it rise for at least 8 but up to 24 hours.

NOTES: I always prefer to measure flour by weight, but this is one time when I super-strongly encourage doing so. No matter how carefully you measure with alternative methods, the only way to be spot on is to use a scale and that seems to make a difference in this recipe. That said, it won't be inedible if you're a bit off on the flour . . . it just may not spread itself quite as easily in the pan.

I also recommend covering the bowl tightly with a double thickness of plastic wrap to avoid attracting fruit flies while the dough is rising. A tight-fitting lid is not a great plan because this bread dough gives off enough gases during the long rise that it has actually blown rigid lids off my containers as it expands.

CLASSIC HOMESTYLE SHEET PAN PIZZA

Everyone has a picture of a perfect pizza in their mind, and for many, it's an old-fashioned Homestyle Sheet Pan Pizza. This is much like the homemade sheet pan pizza my mom used to make almost every week for us when I was growing up, so obviously, the comfort factor of this pizza is almost off the charts for me.

Yield: 1 half-sheet-pan–size pizza

2 tbsp (30 ml) neutral oil (grapeseed, sunflower, canola, or vegetable)

2 tbsp (20 g) cornmeal or semolina

1 half-sheet-pan–size ball of Classic Pizza Dough (page 38)

¾ cup (180 ml) thin pizza sauce

Extra virgin olive oil or Garlic Olive Oil (page 173) for brushing the crust

2 cups (265 g) shredded part-skim mozzarella

½ cup other toppings (like pepperoni, sausage, pan-fried peppers and onions, etc.)

Preheat the oven to 425°F (220°C). Drizzle the neutral oil over a rimmed half sheet pan and scatter the cornmeal or semolina over the oil.

On a baking mat or clean, lightly floured counter, stretch the dough to the approximate size and shape of your half sheet pan. Gently lift the dough onto the prepared pan. If you create any holes while moving the dough, gently pinch them closed. The dough may not completely fill the pan and that is okay. It should fill it most of the way though. Spread the sauce over the dough, leaving ½ inch (13 mm) unsauced around the perimeter of the dough. Brush the perimeter with extra virgin olive oil or Garlic Olive Oil.

Scatter the shredded mozzarella and any other toppings evenly over the crust. Bake for 25 to 30 minutes, or until the crust is set and golden brown around the edges.

NOTES: Feel free to change up your cheese and topping combinations, staying as close to the given amounts as possible. Some of our favorite pizza topping and cheese combinations are:

Barbecue Pulled Pork Pizza: Mix 2 cups (500 g) of pulled pork with ¾ cup (180 ml) of barbecue sauce. Spread the mixture over the crust and top with equal parts mild cheddar and mozzarella. When finished, garnish with sliced green onions.

Buffalo Chicken Pizza: Top the crust with 2 cups (500 g) of leftover cooked chicken tossed with ½ cup (120 ml) of Buffalo sauce and mozzarella cheese. Garnish the baked pizza with minced chives and crumbled bleu cheese.

White Pizza: Mix 2 crushed garlic cloves with 2 cups (500 g) of part-skim ricotta cheese and a handful of chopped fresh parsley. Spread over the crust, top with mozzarella cheese, and bake until the crust is crispy. Garnish the finished pizza with generous amounts of fresh basil.

WOOD-FIRED OR STONE-COOKED PIZZA

The chewy crust with big dough bubbles and light charring on stone-cooked or wood-fired pizzas makes me dizzy with happiness. My Classic Pizza Dough (page 38) is just the thing to create a restaurant-worthy pizza in your own home using either of these cooking methods. The instructions for these two styles of pizza are similar enough to combine into one recipe.

Yield: 1 (12-inch [30-cm]) pizza

Generous amount of cornmeal or semolina for the peel

1 (12-inch [30-cm]) ball of Classic Pizza Dough (page 38)

¼ cup (60 ml) thin pizza sauce

1 cup (133 g) shredded part-skim mozzarella

2 tbsp other toppings (like sausage, pan-fried peppers and onions, etc.) or up to 6 slices of pepperoni

Fresh basil, for garnish after cooking

Preheat your wood-fired oven or a pizza stone in your oven as hot as it will go, preferably 550°F (290°C) or much higher. Scatter a generous layer of cornmeal or semolina over a peel.

On a baking mat or lightly floured counter, gently pat out the ball of dough until it is a disc about ½ inch (13 mm) thick. Place your hand in the center of the disc and spin it, spreading your fingers as you go to stretch it out. When you find you can no longer do this, lift the disc by just inside the edge and let gravity pull it, until you have an approximate circle that is roughly 12 inches (30 cm) in diameter. Take care not to tear the dough. It's better a little thicker than you'd like than torn.

Gently transfer the stretched dough to the peel and gently shimmy the peel to make sure the dough moves freely. If it does not, carefully lift the part that is not moving and add more cornmeal or semolina underneath it until it does. Add the sauce to within ¼ inch (6 mm) of the perimeter, and then shimmy the peel again, shaking after each addition of sauce, cheese, and toppings to be sure it can all still move freely.

Slide the pizza carefully onto the preheated stone or into a wood-fired pizza oven. Check often, starting at 1 minute, for doneness. When the pizza reaches your desired darkness (about 1½ minutes in a wood-fired oven or 8 to 12 minutes on a stone), use the peel to transfer the pizza to a heat-proof cutting board. Tear fresh basil leaves over the pizza to garnish. Let it stand 1 to 3 minutes before slicing.

NOTE: Keep the toppings light. These pizzas can't handle a mega-load of toppings. You're going to be sliding these from a peel onto a screaming-hot stone in your oven or wood-fired pizza oven, and an overloaded crust has a distressing tendency to stick to a peel and flop rather than sliding effortlessly onto the hot stone.

COOL-KITCHEN GRILLED PIZZA

Cravings don't stop just because the weather gets too hot to even consider baking a pizza for dinner. Enter the Cool-Kitchen Grilled Pizza stage left. This pizza hits all the right notes without turning your kitchen into an oven. Top sparingly when you grill this pizza, but hit it with all the garnish you want once it's done!

Yield: 2 (10- to 12-inch [25- to 30-cm]) pizzas

1 tbsp (15 ml) neutral oil (grapeseed, sunflower, canola, or vegetable)

1 (10- or 12-inch [25- or 30-cm]) ball of Classic Pizza Dough (page 38)

3 tbsp (45 ml) extra virgin olive oil or Garlic Olive Oil (page 173), divided

¼ cup (60 ml) thin pizza sauce

1 cup (133 g) shredded part-skim mozzarella or 4 to 5 slices fresh mozzarella

2 tbsp other toppings (like sausage, pan-fried peppers and onions, etc.) or up to 6 slices of pepperoni

Fresh basil and/or thinly sliced prosciutto, for garnish

Prepare your grill for high, direct heat. Make sure your toppings are ready to go. When the grill is hot, use tongs to rub a paper towel soaked with the neutral oil over the grates of the grill.

On a baking mat or lightly floured surface, gently hand stretch or use a rolling pin to roll out your dough to a 10- or 12-inch (25- or 30-cm) oval or circle, depending on the size of your dough ball. Let the dough rest for 5 minutes, then stretch it back if it has shrunk at all. Carefully transfer to a peel or to an upside-down half sheet pan. Brush the surface of the dough with 1½ tablespoons (23 ml) of the olive oil. You can either carefully invert the pan/peel over the grill or use your hands to transfer it, oil-side down. Close the lid of the grill and let the pizza cook for 2 minutes. Open the grill, slide a fish spatula or other flexible spatula under the crust, and rotate the crust 90 degrees. Close the grill and cook for 1 minute, or until the dough is browning underneath and bubbly on top.

Open the grill and brush the dough with the remaining 1½ tablespoons (23 ml) of olive oil, then slide the spatula under the dough and flip it carefully.

Immediately top with the sauce, cheese, and any other toppings you have. Close the grill and cook for 2 to 3 more minutes, or until the cheese is melted and the entire pizza is hot. Remove the pizza using the fish spatula or a peel to slide it onto a cutting board. Garnish with torn basil and/or thin strips of prosciutto, slice, and enjoy!

NOTE: After your grilled pizza is off the heat source, you can top it with just about anything you like. I love topping these grilled pizzas with a combination of fresh herbs and thin slices of prosciutto. When I'm feeling wild and crazy, I've also topped them with arugula lightly dressed in Italian dressing and that is divine!

"I CAN'T BELIEVE THIS IS HOMEMADE" PAN PIZZA

I know the name of this recipe probably sounds like hyperbole, but I promise you it isn't. This is the best pan pizza I've ever had, and it is made not just in my home kitchen, but in the home kitchens of the thousands of Foodie with Family readers who have made it and fallen in love with it. It's so insanely easy and tastes a little reminiscent of Pizza Hut's Personal Pan Pizzas, but oh-so-much better.

Yield: 2 (10- to 12-inch [25- to 30-cm]) skillet pizzas or 3 (8-inch [20-cm]) cake-pan pizzas

4 tbsp (60 ml) neutral oil with a low smoke point (such as grapeseed, sunflower, canola, or vegetable oil), plus extra for your hands

1 batch of risen Best Pan Pizza Dough (page 39)

1½ cups (360 ml) thick pizza sauce

2 cups (265 g) shredded part-skim mozzarella

12 to 16 pieces pepperoni

6 fresh basil leaves, divided (optional but tasty)

NOTES: You can most definitely vary the sauces and toppings you use for this pizza, but try not to overload the crust. You should max out at the recipe's listed amount of sauce, whether it's barbecue sauce, Alfredo sauce, or masala curry sauce. When it comes to toppings, go with no more than about ½ cup of toppings whether it be par-cooked sausage or pancetta, diced cooked chicken, fried onions and peppers, spinach leaves, or whatever you like. Anything more than that amount will keep the crust from cooking all the way through and that would be terribly sad.

Divide the oil evenly between 2 (10- to 12-inch [25- to 30-cm]) heavy, cast-iron skillets (or between 3 [8-inch (20-cm)] cake pans). The heavier the pans are, the better your end result will be. Swirl to coat the bottoms of the pans with the oil.

Oil your hands generously and divide the risen dough into two or three pieces, depending on which pans you're using. Gently form each piece into a ball by pulling the side of the dough and tucking it under, rotating one-quarter turn and repeating the tug and tuck, rotating another one-quarter turn and repeating the tug and tuck, then finally doing it once more to form a loose ball. Lay it smooth-side down in the oil, then flip so the whole thing is coated in oil. Use the palm of your hand to gently flatten the dough. It will not spread to the edges yet, but that is okay. Cover the pan tightly with plastic wrap and set out at room temperature, undisturbed, for 2 hours.

Preheat the oven as high as it will go, preferably to 550°F (290°C), with a pizza stone (if available) on a rack in the lower third of the oven. Remove the plastic wrap from the pans. The dough should have spread itself (or nearly spread itself) to the edges of the pan. Simply lift the edges of dough to pull toward the sides of the pan if necessary. This will help loosen any trapped air under the dough as well. If there are any large air bubbles, nudge them down with the back of a knuckle.

Divide the sauce between the pans and spread right to the edges of the dough. Divide the cheese and top each pizza evenly to the edge, then distribute the pepperoni over the pizzas. If using it, tear half of your basil leaves and toss over the tops of the pizzas. Reserve half of the basil to add to the pizzas when they're removed from the oven.

Put the pans into the hot oven on the stone and bake for 12 to 20 minutes (depending on how well done you want your pizzas). You can check the underside of the pizza crust for doneness by lifting the edge gently with a flexible spatula (like a fish turner). A finished pizza will have a crisp, deep-brown bottom and a bubbly, golden- to deep–golden brown top. I pull my pizzas when the edges have some deeply caramelized (read: lightly charred) edges and some dark brown bubbles on top.

Use a flexible spatula to slide under the pizza and edge it out onto a cutting board. Tear the remaining basil and scatter it over the pizzas. Let rest for 5 minutes before slicing into wedges, then let it rest without moving it for another 3 minutes before serving.

DETROIT-STYLE PIZZA

Detroit-Style Pizza is a chewy, deep-dish crust with a super crisp bottom and crispy, lacey, ever-so-slightly blackened edges on the generous amounts of cheese. This is a pizza of the people and boy is it good. It's maybe a little less well known than Chicago-style deep dish, but its day is coming. Trust me; it is just so good. It may seem a little weird to dollop the sauce over the cheese rather than under it, but one bite and you'll be a believer. Long live Detroit and its pizza!

Yield: 1 large pizza with 8 very generous-size rectangular slices

2 tbsp (30 ml) neutral oil (refined olive, canola, sunflower, or grapeseed oil) plus extra for your hands

1 batch risen Best Pan Pizza Dough (page 39)

24 slices pepperoni

8 oz (227 g) Monterey Jack or block Muenster cheese, cut into ½-inch (13-mm) cubes

4 oz (113 g) part-skim mozzarella cheese, grated

¾ cup (180 ml) thick pizza sauce

Pour the oil into a metal 9 x 13-inch (23 x 33-cm) pan and swirl to cover the bottom with oil.

Oil your hands generously and gently form the dough into a ball by pulling the side of the dough and tucking it under, rotating one-quarter turn and repeating the tug and tuck, rotating another one-quarter turn and repeating the tug and tuck, then finally doing it once more to form a loose ball. Lay it smooth-side down in the oil, then flip so the whole thing is coated in oil. Use the palm of your hand to gently flatten the dough. It will not spread to the edges yet, but that is okay. Cover the pan tightly with plastic wrap and set out at room temperature, undisturbed, for 2 hours.

Preheat the oven as high as it will go, preferably to 550°F (290°C), with a pizza stone (if available) on the top rack to help radiate heat evenly through the oven; make sure there is enough room to put your pan directly on the floor of your oven.

Remove the plastic wrap from the pan. The dough should now have spread itself (or nearly spread itself) to the edges of the pan. Simply lift the edges of dough to pull toward the sides of the pan if necessary. This will help loosen any trapped air under the dough as well. If there are any large air bubbles, nudge them down with the back of a knuckle.

Arrange 12 of the slices of pepperoni directly on the dough in three by four rows, and scatter both types of cheese evenly over the dough, making sure you get cheese all the way up against the edges. Arrange the remaining 12 slices of pepperoni over the cheese in three by four rows. Dollop the sauce between the pepperoni slices. Place the pan directly on the floor of the oven and bake for 13 to 18 minutes, depending on how well done you like the top of your pizza.

You can check the underside of the pizza crust for doneness by lifting the edge gently with a flexible spatula (like a fish turner). A finished pizza will have a crisp, deep-brown bottom and a bubbly, golden- to deep-golden brown top.

Use a flexible spatula to slide under the pizza and edge it out onto a cutting board. Let rest for 5 minutes before slicing in half lengthwise, then four times across, yielding eight rectangular pieces of pizza. Let the pizza rest without moving it for another 3 minutes before serving.

NOTES

You absolutely, positively need to use a metal pan for a Detroit-Style Pizza, and preferably a carbon or anodized steel pan, aluminized steel pan, or cast-iron pan. Do not under any circumstances use glass. It will break at the temperatures needed to make this pizza.

I know it sounds a little nutty to put the pizza directly on the floor of the oven, but stay with me on this. The floor of the oven is the hottest part of most home ovens, and you want to get a super crispy crust. This is a very wet dough, and that extra burst of heat from the floor does magic for it.

Monterey Jack and Muenster cheese are both very creamy and buttery and are good melters. You can swap in all mozzarella for the generous 12 ounces (340 g) of cheese, but you'll be missing a little bit of the butteriness Detroit Pizzas are known for having if you do.

"CHOOSE YOUR OWN ADVENTURE" MEAT-AND-CHEESE CALZONES

Calzones are basically a portable, hand-held pizza pocket. One could argue that pizza is hand-held anyway, but it's awfully hard to eat a slice of pizza and drive a car in rush hour at the same time. A calzone, on the other hand, is tidy, easy to hold in one hand, and almost endlessly customizable. Like traditional calzone recipes, I opt to leave sauce out of the pizza pocket and save it for dipping. I find the crust more consistently done when the sauce is for dunking rather than part of the package. You can use just about any fully cooked meat or vegetable-and-cheese combination you love from Buffalo chicken and Jack cheese to roast beef and provolone to ham and Swiss. These calzones are a great way to use up odds and ends from the fridge. See the filling ideas for some quick and easy combos you'll love.

Yield: 2 single serving-size calzones

2 (10-inch [25-cm]) balls Classic Pizza Dough (page 38)

1 cup (130 g) chopped, fully cooked meat or vegetables

1 cup (113 g) grated cheese

3 green onions, sliced

1 egg, beaten

1 tbsp (15 ml) water

Preheat the oven to 450°F (230°C). Line a rimmed half sheet pan with parchment paper or a silicone baking mat.

Working with one dough ball at a time on a silicone baking mat on the counter or on a clean counter, use your hands to gently flatten the ball into a disc. Use a rolling pin to ease the dough into a circle that is 8 to 10 inches (20 to 25 cm) in diameter. Let the dough rest while you assemble the filling.

Toss the meat or vegetables with the grated cheese and sliced green onions. In a small mixing bowl, whisk together the egg and water.

If the dough rounds have shrunk slightly, gently coax them back to the original size as you move them to the prepared pan. Brush the dough lightly with a little of the egg wash all the way to the edges, and mound half of the filling over a half moon of the dough, leaving about ½ inch (13 mm) of dough unfilled around the perimeter. Lift the excess dough and drape it over the filling, tucking in any that threatens to escape. Pinch and crimp the edges of the calzones to seal. Brush all over lightly with more of the egg wash.

Use a sharp knife to cut two or three vent holes on the top of each calzone, making sure to expose the filling as you do so. This will prevent soggy calzones.

Bake for 15 minutes, or until the crust is a beautiful, deep golden brown and firm. Let the calzones rest on the pan for 5 minutes, then for another 5 minutes to allow the crust to set up. Serve with the dip of your choice.

FILLING IDEAS

Here are some of our favorite filling and dip combinations that make using up leftovers a snap.

Ham and Cheese Calzone: chopped ham with cheddar, Swiss, or mozzarella and green onions. Use marinara sauce for dip.

Buffalo Chicken Calzone: Buffalo chicken (page 40) plus Monterey Jack and crumbled bleu cheese, and chopped chives with bleu cheese or ranch dressing for dip. Pssst. The answer is only bleu cheese in Buffalo, NY.

Roast Beef Dinner Calzone: sliced roast beef, chopped and tossed with diced provolone cheese, 2 tablespoons (28 g) of caramelized onions, and 1 tablespoon (15 ml) of grainy mustard. Serve with horseradish sauce or creamy mustard sauce for dip.

Cheeseburger Calzone: chopped, leftover burgers tossed with grated cheddar cheese and a teaspoon each of ketchup and mustard. If you have some leftover bacon, chop that and toss it in, too. Serve with your favorite barbecue sauce or Thousand Island dressing as dip.

Mushroom Lover's Calzone: leftover seared mushrooms, caramelized onions, and provolone cheese. Serve with warm marinara sauce or barbecue sauce for dip.

Broccoli and Goat Cheese Calzone: leftover roasted broccoli, roughly chopped, mixed with 3 to 6 ounces (85 to 170 g) of garlic and herb goat cheese, a dash of crushed red pepper flakes, and green onions. Serve plain or dunk in marinara sauce.

BETTER-THAN-PIZZERIA GARLIC KNOTS

If you are one of those people with a will of steel who can walk past a warm bowl of garlic knots without eating any, I applaud you. And you confuse me. Garlic knots are basically everything good in one package. They're bread slathered with garlic oil and herbs and (if you're fortunate) Parmesan cheese that are meant to be eaten warm. I could probably eat these almost every day and be a happy woman. They're made with our Classic Pizza Dough (page 38), so if you have a batch hanging out in the refrigerator, you can have these on the table in about an hour and a half!

Yield: 12 garlic knots

1 sheet pan pizza–size ball of Classic Pizza Dough (page 38), brought to room temperature for about an hour

6 tbsp (90 ml) Garlic Olive Oil (page 173)

2 cloves garlic, peeled and pressed or minced

¾ tsp Italian seasoning blend

½ tsp kosher salt

½ cup (40 g) grated shake-on-style Parmesan cheese

Marinara sauce, for serving (optional)

Line a baking sheet or half sheet pan with parchment paper or a silicone baking mat. Set aside.

Cut the pizza dough into twelve equal pieces. Roll each piece into a 6- to 8-inch (15- to 20-cm)–long rope. Cross the ends of the dough over each other and tie into a simple knot. Place each knot on the lined sheet pan, leaving at least 2 inches (5 cm) of space between them. Cover the pan with a clean, dry towel and let the knots rise while the oven preheats to 400°F (200°C), about 20 to 30 minutes.

Stir together the Garlic Olive Oil, garlic, Italian seasoning, and salt. After the oven has heated up fully, uncover the knotted dough and brush lightly with approximately half of the garlic oil mixture. Bake for 15 to 20 minutes, or until the dough is golden brown and set. Brush the garlic knots generously with the remaining garlic oil, then sprinkle the Parmesan on with abandon. Serve warm as is or with a bowl of warmed marinara sauce.

NOTE: For mouth-watering rosemary garlic knots, swap an equal quantity of dried rosemary for the Italian seasoning blend.

BAKERY-STYLE CIABATTA LOAVES OR ROLLS

Ciabatta kind of looks like an accident; like a bread that gave up halfway, doesn't it? But that slumpy, flat, misshapen loaf is one of the best things *ever* for sopping up sauces or splitting and filling with the best sandwich fixings. One of my all-time favorite sandwiches from my Foodie with Family blog is a ciabatta roll, split and toasted, filled with grilled chicken, and topped with marinara sauce, pesto, and copious amounts of melted mozzarella. Our crazy-simple Best Pan Pizza Dough (page 39) just happens to be the right amount of slack and wet to make a chewy, holey, and simple ciabatta.

Yield: 3 medium loaves or 12 sandwich-size rolls

¾ cup (94 g) all-purpose flour

¾ cup (125 g) semolina flour

1 batch risen Best Pan Pizza Dough (page 39)

Line a sheet pan with parchment paper or a silicone baking mat. Use a fork to mix together the all-purpose flour and semolina flour in a mixing bowl. Sprinkle a generous ½ cup (73 g) of the mixture over the pan and set aside.

Scatter a generous ½ cup (73 g) of the flour mixture over a silicone mat on the counter or a clean counter. Flip the container of dough upside down onto the counter and allow gravity to pull the dough out. Do not punch down or knock back the dough. Handle it as gently as possible to keep as much air in it as you can.

Scrape out any dough that remains and sprinkle the rest of the flour mixture over the dough. Use a bench knife or dough scraper to gently nudge the dough into a square. Using the bench knife or dough scraper again, cut the dough into three equal rectangles by pushing the blade straight down into the dough. If you're going to make rolls, cut each rectangle crosswise into four pieces.

Use the bench knife and your hands to transfer each rectangle of dough to the prepared pan, leaving about 2 to 3 inches (5 to 8 cm) between each piece. Drape a piece of plastic wrap over the dough and let it rest while you preheat the oven to 425°F (220°C).

When the oven reaches temperature, bake the loaves for 25 minutes or the rolls for 20 minutes, or until they are a deep golden brown and sound hollow when they're tapped. Remove the pan and transfer the ciabatta or rolls to a rack to cool completely before slicing.

Italian-Style
SEMOLINA
BREAD DOUGH

I think this is my favorite dough to work with in the entire book. It's supple, versatile, and makes so many tasty things.

Even if you think you've never tried semolina flour, I guarantee you have. It's the same flour that makes most dried Italian pastas and couscous. It's extremely high in protein and gluten, which translates to a finished bread that is chewy, higher rising, and beautiful in structure. Its light yellow color tends to make a pretty bread.

Semolina flour is found in most moderately well-stocked grocery stores on the shelves near the regular flour, specialty flours, or in the health food section. It's also readily available from Internet retailers, which is how I usually get mine. I try to keep this on hand in abundance all the time.

The Braided Italian Bread (page 58) made from this dough is my kids' all-time favorite bread. Knowing a batch of this bread is going with dinner is enough to make them grin from ear to ear. And if I let them tear off sections of these loaves when they're still warm from the oven, it will turn around their worst bad days. For a bread that looks so impressive, it's remarkably easy to make.

While that one bread is reason enough to include the dough in this book, the Ham and Cheese Rolls (page 61) and Barbecue Bacon Cheeseburger Stuffed Rolls (page 62) are hand-held meals to please all ages. They make great lunch-bag additions or can be served alongside a tossed salad for a casual meal that is satisfying and exciting.

Jalapeño Cheddar Bread (page 65), Individual Garlic Braids (page 69), Kalamata Olive Stuffed Rolls (page 73), and Sun-Dried Tomato Pesto Pinwheel Rolls (page 70) are what I like to call snackable breads; they are easy to tear or slice and just eat alone, but they also all make great bases for sandwiches or accompaniments to salads or soups. When you see how beautiful they are, you're definitely going to want to pat yourself on the back. They're so simple, but so stunning and tantalizing, too.

Each of these breads made with the semolina bread dough smells so good while they're baking that you'll be hard pressed to wait. Thankfully they're the best suited recipes for tearing into with your hands or teeth while they're still quite warm. Be aware that if you opt for doing that you will want to eat the entire whole loaf in one sitting. If you let them cool well before slicing, though, they're good for a couple of days.

BRAIDED ITALIAN BREAD

This chewy but tender Italian-style bread is a thing of beauty: golden brown, crispy crust topped with crunchy seeds (and perhaps spices) and a soft, yielding interior. This is one of the easiest doughs in creation to work with and creates a bread of beauty that will impress everyone!

Yield: 2 loaves

SEMOLINA BREAD DOUGH

4 cups (1 lb, 1 oz [482 g], by weight) all-purpose flour

2 cups (11.5 oz [326 g], by weight) semolina flour

3 tsp (12 g) SAF° or instant yeast

3 tsp (18 g) kosher salt

4 tbsp (50 g) sugar

4 tbsp (60 ml) extra virgin olive oil

2 cups (480 ml) lukewarm water

1 beaten egg

OPTIONAL TOPPINGS

Sesame seeds

Poppy seeds

Onion flakes, dehydrated

Garlic flakes, dehydrated

NOTE: My personal favorite toppings for this bread are simple sesame seeds or a blend of dehydrated garlic and onion flakes with sesame seeds and poppy seeds, much like our Everything Bagel Topping (page 172) without the salt. It is also good without any toppings at all, in all its shiny, brown glory.

Add the all-purpose flour, semolina flour, yeast, salt, sugar, olive oil, and water to a large mixing bowl or the bowl of a stand mixer and stir with a sturdy wooden spoon until a shaggy but cohesive dough comes together. Knead by hand or with the dough hook on a stand mixer until the dough is smooth and elastic, about 10 minutes. Scrape the bowl clean with a dough scraper, form a tight round of dough, and return it to the bowl. Cover with a shower cap or plastic wrap, and let rise in a warm, draft-free place until doubled in size, about 2 hours.

Turn the dough out onto a clean surface and divide the dough in half, then divide each half into three pieces. Set aside and cover three of the pieces with a towel while working with the others.

Pat one piece of dough into a rough oval. Use the side of your hand to press an indentation along the length of the dough piece. Fold the dough together along the length of the indentation and roll lightly with your hands to form a thick rope between 12 and 14 inches (30 and 36 cm) long. Repeat with the other two pieces so that you have three ropes of roughly equal length. Line them up in parallel with the ends facing you.

Gently grasp the end of the rope on the far left. Lift it to about the center, leaving the far end still on the counter, cross it over the rope nearest to it, and lay it down. Now grasp the end of the piece on the far right and lift it to about the center, leaving its far end on the counter, cross it over the (now) center rope (which is the first one you moved), and lay it down. This is the maneuver you will repeat—far left over center, far right over center, and so on—until you have ends too short to continue. At that point, pinch the ends together and tuck under the braid. Now go back to the center of the loaf and finish braiding the loaf toward the top. When you reach the ends, pinch together and tuck under. Repeat this process with the other three pieces of dough. Cover the loaves lightly and let rise in a warm place until puffy in appearance and roughly doubled in size, about 30 minutes.

Preheat the oven to 400°F (200°C). Whisk the egg until very loose. Paint the egg generously onto the risen bread braids and sprinkle the braids with the desired toppings.

Bake for 18 to 26 minutes or until the loaves are your preferred shade of golden to deep brown and firm on top. Turn the oven off, prop the door open a little (2 inches [5 cm], if you can make your door behave), and let cool for at least an hour. Or tear into the loaves with your teeth. I won't tell.

HAM AND CHEESE ROLLS

For these Ham and Cheese Rolls: our beautiful semolina bread dough is wrapped around classic smoked deli ham, loads of shredded cheddar, and just enough chopped green onions to keep things interesting before it is sliced into rolls and baked to perfection. These rolls are ready to unwind—or bite straight through the pinwheel of tender bread, hot salty ham, and melted, gooey cheesy perfection; whichever suits your fancy.

Yield: about 16 rolls

1 batch Semolina Bread Dough (page 58)

8 oz (227 g) cheddar cheese, grated, divided

19 slices deli ham

1 bunch green onions, green parts only, thinly sliced

Roll out the bread dough until it is a 24 x 18-inch (61 x 46–cm) rectangle. Sprinkle about a quarter of the cheese over the surface of the dough. Lay out the ham slices in overlapping rows to cover all but 1 inch (3 cm) along the 24-inch (61-cm) side nearest you.

Scatter the remaining grated cheese and green onions over the ham. Gently roll the farthest edge onto itself and roll up toward you. Pinch the seams together and slice into 1½- to 2-inch (4- to 5-cm) rounds. Arrange on a Silpat- or parchment-lined half sheet pan. Cover with a clean tea towel and let rise for about 45 minutes, or until puffy looking.

Preheat the oven to 400°F (200°C). Remove the towel and bake for 20 to 25 minutes or until deep golden brown. Let the rolls stand for 5 minutes before transferring to a rack or serving plate.

NOTE: These rolls can be individually wrapped and frozen. See instructions on freezing and defrosting breads (page 177) for best results.

BARBECUE BACON CHEESEBURGER STUFFED ROLLS

This is my youngest son's favorite recipe in the entire cookbook. He says it may even be one of the best things I've ever made. These portable, sealed (well, until you bite into them), hand-held, crowd-pleasing buns are stuffed full of browned ground beef and crispy bacon in a cheesy barbecue sauce. Served with a salad, you have a complete meal guaranteed to bring smiles. These buns freeze and thaw like a dream, too. See the Notes below the recipe for instructions on stashing away some of this happiness in the freezer.

Yield: 8 stuffed buns

1 lb (454 g) 90% lean ground beef

12 slices crispy bacon, crumbled or cut into thin strips

8 oz (227 g) shredded Monterey Jack or pepper Jack cheese

½ cup (120 ml) barbecue sauce

½ batch risen Semolina Bread Dough (page 58; see Notes)

1 egg, beaten

1 tbsp (15 ml) water

Sesame seeds

Brown the ground beef in a pan over medium–high heat, breaking it up with a spatula or spoon as you go. When there is no longer any pinkness left to the meat, drain any fat and transfer to a mixing bowl. Stir in the bacon, cheese, and barbecue sauce until evenly mixed.

Line a half sheet pan with a silicone baking mat or parchment paper. Set aside.

On a clean counter or a counter covered with a silicone baking mat, divide the dough into eight equal pieces. Roll each piece into a tight ball and set aside, covering the rolls with a towel to keep them from drying out. Roll one piece at a time into a round that is 5 to 6 inches (13 to 15 cm) in diameter. Scoop about ¼ cup (55 g) of the beef filling into the center of the round. Gather up the edges around the filling and pinch to seal. Place seam-side down on the prepared pan, leaving 2 to 3 inches (5 to 8 cm) between the buns. Repeat with the remaining dough and filling.

Cover the buns with a damp tea towel and put in a warm, draft-free place to rise while you preheat the oven to 400°F (200°C). When the oven is ready, whisk together the egg and water and brush the surface of the buns generously with the mixture. Sprinkle with sesame seeds and bake for 18 to 24 minutes, or until the rolls are a glossy, deep golden brown color. Let the rolls rest on the pan for 5 minutes before transferring to a cooling rack. Allow them to cool for another 15 minutes before eating.

NOTES: You can use the other half of the batch of semolina dough to make a loaf of Braided Italian Bread (page 58) or the Taco Dinner Braid (page 66).

If you'd like to freeze these buns for later, you can let them cool completely on the cooling rack, then follow the instructions on freezing bread (page 177) for the best results. To defrost and reheat the buns, follow these instructions: Take the desired number of buns from the freezer and place in a cold oven on a sheet pan still wrapped in their foil. Set the temperature of the oven to 250°F (130°C). When the oven reaches the correct temperature, continue to bake for 10 to 20 minutes, or until warmed through.

JALAPEÑO CHEDDAR BREAD

Jalapeño Cheddar Bread is a soft, tender-but-sturdy-enough-for-sandwiches bread made from our soft Braided Italian Bread (page 58) with a cap of melted, crisped cheddar cheese. Under that beautiful, golden brown top is bread swirled with thin slices of fresh jalapeño and more cheddar cheese that melts into the loaf as it bakes. This is seriously good stuff. One of my sons ate an entire loaf of it in one sitting by himself. I won't say he was entirely free of regret when he was done, but he maintains it was worth it.

Yield: 2 loaves

Nonstick cooking spray

1 batch risen Semolina Bread Dough (page 58)

8 oz (227 g) extra-sharp cheddar, grated, divided

3 small- to medium-size fresh jalapeños, stems removed, sliced into ⅛-inch (3-mm)-thick rounds, divided

Spray two loaf pans with nonstick cooking spray and set them aside.

Divide the dough into two pieces. Working with one piece of dough at a time, pat into an oval, then use a rolling pin to roll it into a rectangle that is approximately 8 x 14 inches (20 x 36 cm). Sprinkle one-third of the grated cheese and one-third of the jalapeño rounds over the rectangle. Roll it up from a short side. As you roll, keep the dough tight against itself, trying to avoid stretching it more. Pinch the seams, tuck the ends under, and place seam-side down on the prepared pan. Repeat with the second piece of dough.

Toss the remaining grated cheese and jalapeño slices together and distribute evenly over the tops of the two loaves. Cover with a damp tea towel and let rise in a warm, draft-free place until they are puffy, about 30 minutes. While they rise, preheat the oven to 400°F (200°C). Bake the loaves for 25 to 30 minutes, or until deep golden brown and firm on top. Let the bread rest in the pans for 3 minutes after they're removed from the oven before turning out onto a cooling rack. Cool completely before slicing.

TACO DINNER BRAID

If the Bible had a loaves and taco story, this recipe would be featured in it. You take 3 cups (750 g) of leftover taco meat or pulled pork or chicken, a couple of cups of grated cheese, some chopped green onions, and half a batch of bread dough and turn it into a meal that can feed a bunch of hungry teenage boys. We serve this with a hearty helping of salsa and some guacamole and call it a meal!

Yield: 1 large stuffed, braided bread; 6 servings

3 cups (750 g) leftover taco meat, pulled pork, or shredded chicken

8 oz (227 g) shredded cheddar or pepper Jack cheese

5 green onions, thinly sliced

3 tbsp (45 ml) taco sauce

½ batch Semolina Bread Dough (page 58)

1 egg, beaten

Salsa and guacamole, for serving (optional)

Preheat the oven to 400°F (200°C). Line a rimmed half sheet pan with parchment paper or a silicone baking mat. Set aside.

In a medium-size mixing bowl, stir together the taco meat, cheddar cheese, green onions, and taco sauce.

On a counter covered with a silicone baking mat or lightly floured surface, roll out the semolina dough into a rectangle that is about 15 x 13 inches (38 x 33 cm). Transfer the rectangle to the prepared pan.

Spoon the filling down the center of the rectangle in a 6-inch (15-cm)–wide strip. Using a sharp knife, make cuts 1 inch (3 cm) apart (perpendicular to the filling) on each long side of the rectangle to within ½ inch (13 mm) of the filling. Fold the strips of dough diagonally over the filling, alternating between the left side and the right side and pressing to seal. Brush with the beaten egg.

Bake for 25 to 33 minutes, or until the bread is deep golden brown and the filling is set. Place the pan on a cooling rack and let it rest for 5 to 10 minutes before slicing. Serve with salsa and guacamole, if desired.

INDIVIDUAL GARLIC BRAIDS

Bread makes me happy. Garlic bread makes me happier. Individual garlic bread makes me even happier than that, but individual garlic bread that is braided makes me happiest of all. It's better than a hat trick, it's: a) bread, b) extra tasty bread, c) cute bread, and d) cute bread to the fiftieth power. If you're like us, you'll never find yourself with leftovers, but if you do somehow manage not to eat all of them the day they're made, I imagine leftovers would make a nice small sandwich when split lengthwise.

Yield: 6 individual serving-size braids

1 batch risen Semolina Bread Dough (page 58)

⅓ cup (80 ml) Garlic Olive Oil (page 173) or extra virgin olive oil

½ tsp granulated garlic or 1 clove minced fresh garlic

1 tsp dried Italian seasoning

½ tsp kosher salt

Line a half sheet pan with parchment paper or a silicone baking mat. Set it aside.

Turn the dough out onto a counter covered with a silicone baking mat or a lightly floured surface. Divide the dough into six equal pieces. Cover all but one piece with a tea towel.

Divide the uncovered dough into three equal pieces and roll each piece out into a rope that is between 10 and 12 inches (25 and 30 cm) long. Braid these pieces using the instructions found in the Braided Italian Bread (page 58). Place the braid on the prepared pan. Repeat with the remaining five pieces of bread. Arrange the finished braids on the prepared pan leaving 2 to 3 inches (5 to 8 cm) between each braid. Cover the pan with a damp tea towel and set in a warm, draft-free place while you preheat the oven to 400°F (200°C).

In a small bowl, stir together the olive oil, garlic, Italian seasoning blend, and salt. Brush the braids with half of the oil mixture. Bake the braids for 18 to 20 minutes or until they are a deep golden brown. Remove the pan from the oven and brush with the remaining oil mixture. Let them cool at least 5 minutes before serving, and completely if you plan to slice them.

SUN-DRIED TOMATO PESTO PINWHEEL ROLLS

This was, shockingly, my 17-year-old son's favorite recipe in the entire cookbook. This was surprising because in general, this young man still doesn't want to be in the same room as a vegetable unless it has been pureed into pizza or spaghetti sauce; no chunks please. But these rolls stuffed with sun-dried tomato pesto? He couldn't get enough of them. Okay, the pesto is mostly smooth, but there were recognizable pieces of tomato skin. Behold, the power of amazing bread and delicious flavors.

Yield: 12 rolls

Nonstick cooking spray or olive oil

1 batch risen Semolina Bread Dough (page 58)

¾ to 1 cup (190 to 250 g) Sun-Dried Tomato Pesto (page 174)

1 cup (80 g) shredded Parmesan cheese

3 fresh basil leaves, torn

Use nonstick cooking spray or brush olive oil into two 10- to 12-inch (25- to 30-cm) cast-iron skillets or three 8-inch (20-cm) round cake pans. Set them aside.

On a lightly floured surface, roll the dough into a rectangle that is about 24 x 18 inches (61 x 46 cm). Spread the pesto over the surface of the bread dough, leaving about 1 inch (3 cm) of one long edge clean.

Gently but firmly roll the dough, beginning at the long edge that is spread with pesto, jelly-roll style, until you reach the clean edge. Pinch the dough together at the seam. It may not hold together completely, but that is okay. Lay the tube seam-side down and cut first in half, then cut each half into six equally sized rounds for a total of twelve rolls. Put them into the prepared pans (six rolls in each skillet pan or four rolls in each cake pan).

Cover with a piece of plastic wrap and set aside for 20 minutes in a warm, draft-free place while the oven preheats to 400°F (200°C).

Bake the rolls for 18 to 24 minutes, or until completely set and rich golden brown. Sprinkle the Parmesan cheese and basil evenly over the rolls. Allow the rolls to cool in the pans for 10 minutes before sliding a flexible spatula into the pan and easing them onto a rack. They can be eaten warm or cooled and stored tightly wrapped in the refrigerator for up to 3 days. These are best eaten reheated if they've been refrigerated.

NOTE: To reheat, place a roll in a paper bag, close the bag and roll the top down one or two times to hold it shut, and microwave in 15-second bursts until the roll is as warm or hot as desired.

KALAMATA OLIVE STUFFED ROLLS

My friend Kim loves olives so much that she named her daughter Olive. Well, to be honest, I'm not sure that her love of the salty little morsels was the only inspiration behind her daughter's name, but it sure didn't hurt. And she loved these rolls a lot, too. Her only request was that there be more olives in them, so here they are, new and improved with another handful of olives thrown in for Olive and her mama. You can eat them warm with meals or as snacks or wait until they're completely cooled and split them for incredible sandwiches.

Yield: 16 rolls

1 batch unrisen Semolina Bread Dough (page 58)

2 cups (270 g) pitted Kalamata olives, coarsely chopped

When you have almost finished kneading the semolina bread, use a machine or your hands to knead the chopped olives into it. Roll the dough into a tight ball and place in a clean bowl. Cover with a piece of plastic wrap, shower cap, or damp tea towel and let rise in a warm, draft-free place until doubled in bulk, 1½ to 2 hours.

Line two rimmed sheet pans with parchment paper or silicone baking mats.

Turn the dough out onto the counter and divide into sixteen equal-size pieces. Roll each piece into a tight round. Arrange eight rolls per sheet pan and space them 2 to 3 inches (5 to 8 cm) apart. Cover loosely with plastic wrap or a tea towel and set in a warm, draft-free place to rise for 20 minutes while the oven preheats to 400°F (200°C).

Bake the rolls for 20 to 23 minutes, or until the rolls are golden brown and firm to the touch. Remove the pan from the oven and place it on a cooling rack for 5 minutes. After 5 minutes, transfer the rolls from the pan to the cooling rack to finish cooling. These can be eaten warm or cooled completely to be sliced for sandwiches.

NOTE: Because of the olives in the rolls, these are not suitable to be stored at room temperature for more than 4 days. If you need to store the rolls longer than 4 days, follow the instructions on freezing and defrosting bread (page 177) for best results.

ENGLISH MUFFIN DOUGH:

Nooks and Crannies for Days

English muffin dough makes English muffin bread and that definitely holds the distinction of being the bread that has been eaten in the highest quantities in my house. If you consider that we're a household that fluctuates between being a five- and eight-person crew, all of whom really love bread, that's saying something meaningful.

What makes this bread so special? It's a no-knead, one-bowl wonder that kids can actually make for themselves, and it doesn't require anything more than ingredients you can find at most convenience stores, a big old bowl with a sturdy spoon, and a couple of loaf pans.

We most often make it "plain" because it makes the most magnificent toast as a base for crispy-edged fried eggs, or a platform for strawberry jam or butter and honey. Because English muffin bread is so versatile, though, we also have a Cinnamon English Muffin Bread (page 79) and a Sausage and Cheese English Muffin Bread (page 80) version. This is because texturally, it's quite similar to English muffins. You grease and dust the pans with cornmeal before the dough goes in, giving it that characteristic crust of classic English muffins. The bread itself is full of the "nooks and crannies" that you love and want. When the bread is almost done, you brush melted butter lavishly over the top, which helps brown the crust to a gorgeous deep golden color. Just in case that isn't enough to convince you, once you turn the bread out onto a cooling rack, you brush it all over with more melted butter.

The hardest part of the entire recipe is waiting for the bread to cool before slicing into it. This is one bread where waiting to slice into it is non-negotiable or the texture will really suffer and you'll be sad.

The recipe yields two loaves that hold up quite nicely in the freezer if you think you won't eat them before they start getting stale. The leftovers of English muffin bread also make excellent breadcrumbs (page 153) for cooking and English Muffin Pizzas (page 157).

You can make proper English Muffins (page 83) with the dough, too, and oh what English muffins they are! You will be hard pressed to go back to the store-bought ones after trying the ones you've made in your own kitchen with this recipe.

TOASTABLE ENGLISH MUFFIN BREAD

To say my family eats a lot of this bread is to undersell it massively. These loaves capture everything you love about English muffins in a convenient, sliceable package. This is a bread that screams "Toast me!" and has all the requisite "nooks and crannies" for pooling warm, melted butter and strawberry jam or sopping up an egg yolk from a fried egg. We even use thick slices for homemade English Muffin Pizzas (page 157) on nights when our schedule is a little nutty.

Yield: 2 loaves

5¾ cups (1 lb, 9 oz [709 g], by weight) all-purpose or bread flour (see Notes)

2¾ cups (660 ml) warm water

1 tbsp (18 g) kosher salt

1 tbsp plus 1½ tsp (19 g) granulated sugar

1 tbsp plus 1¼ tsp (17 g) active dry or instant yeast

Nonstick cooking spray

Cornmeal

⅓ cup (80 ml) melted butter, divided

In a large mixing bowl, stir together the flour, water, salt, sugar, and yeast with a sturdy spoon or dough whisk until it is evenly moist with no dry pockets. The dough will be shaggy and very sticky. Spray a piece of plastic wrap with nonstick cooking spray and lay it loosely over the mixing bowl. Place the bowl in a warm, draft-free place until the dough looks puffy and bubbly, and has risen to about double its original size, about an hour.

While the dough rises, spray two loaf pans with nonstick cooking spray and sprinkle in a fistful of cornmeal. Tilt the pans, tapping gently, until the cornmeal coats the sides and bottoms of the pans, tapping out any excess cornmeal.

Use nonstick cooking spray to generously grease your hands, and divide the dough between the two prepared pans. The pans should be no more than halfway full. If needed, prepare one more loaf pan to hold any excess dough.

Cover the pans loosely with oiled plastic wrap and let rise in a warm, draft-free place until the dough is once again bubbly and puffy looking and just peeking above the edges of the pans, about 30 minutes. While the dough is rising, preheat the oven to 350°F (177°C).

Place the pans on the center rack in the oven and bake for 30 minutes. After 30 minutes, brush the surface of the bread generously with about half of the melted butter, then return the pans to the oven and bake 10 more minutes.

Immediately turn the loaves onto a cooling rack and brush all of the surfaces generously with the remaining melted butter. Cool completely before slicing or the texture will be compromised.

NOTES: I often make this bread with a mixture of half bread flour and half all-purpose flour. I like what it does for the bread texturally. You can substitute 1 cup (120 g) of whole wheat flour for 1 cup (125 g) of the all-purpose or bread flour if you'd like a whole-grain English muffin bread. It may take just slightly longer to rise.

This bread is a great one to freeze. See instructions on freezing and defrosting bread (page 177) for best results.

CINNAMON ENGLISH MUFFIN BREAD

Sometimes you just want something sweet, right? This Cinnamon English Muffin Bread hits all the same happy notes as English Muffin Bread but brings some just-sweet-enough cinnamon baking morsels to the party. While you can certainly toast this in the toaster, do yourself a favor and toast it in a little melted butter in a frying pan. You may never look back at your toaster again.

Yield: 2 loaves

5¾ cups (1 lb, 9 oz [709 g], by weight) all-purpose or bread flour (see Notes on page 76)

2¾ cups (660 ml) warm water

1 cup (168 g) cinnamon baking bits

1 tbsp (18 g) kosher salt

1 tbsp plus 1½ tsp (19 g) granulated sugar

1 tbsp plus 1¼ tsp (17 g) active dry or instant yeast

Nonstick cooking spray

Cornmeal

⅓ cup (80 ml) melted butter, divided

In a large mixing bowl, stir together the flour, water, cinnamon bits, salt, sugar, and yeast with a sturdy spoon or dough whisk until the mixture is evenly moist with no dry pockets. The dough will be shaggy and very sticky. Spray a piece of plastic wrap with nonstick cooking spray and lay it loosely over the mixing bowl. Place the bowl in a warm, draft-free place until the dough looks puffy and bubbly, and has risen to about double its original size, about an hour.

While the dough rises, spray two loaf pans with nonstick cooking spray and sprinkle in a fistful of cornmeal. Tilt the pans, tapping gently, until the cornmeal coats the sides and bottoms of the pans, tapping out any excess cornmeal. Use oil or nonstick cooking spray to generously grease your hands, and divide the dough between the two prepared pans. The pans should be no more than halfway full. If needed, prepare one more loaf pan to hold any excess dough.

Cover the pans loosely with oiled plastic wrap and let the dough rise in a warm, draft-free place until it is once again bubbly and puffy looking and just peeking above the edges of the pans, about 30 minutes. While the dough is rising, preheat the oven to 350°F (177°C).

Place the pans on the center rack in the oven and bake for 30 minutes. After 30 minutes, brush the surface of the bread generously with about half of the melted butter, then return the pans to the oven and bake 10 more minutes.

Immediately turn the loaves onto a cooling rack and brush all of the surfaces generously with the remaining melted butter. Cool completely before slicing or the texture will be compromised.

SAUSAGE AND CHEESE ENGLISH MUFFIN BREAD

You know those sausage, cheese and egg muffin breakfast sandwiches you can get at fast-food joints? This bread is like those, but infinitely better. You bake the sausage and cheese right into the bread, slice it into thick slabs, toast it in butter in a frying pan, and then fry your egg in the same pan. If you'd like to take it up to the next level of heavenly, you can absolutely drape another piece of cheese over the fried egg before sandwiching it between slices of this incredible bread.

Yield: 2 loaves

5¾ cups (1 lb, 9 oz [709 g], by weight) all-purpose or bread flour (see Notes)

2¾ cups (660 ml) warm water

1½ cups (195 g) cooked breakfast sausage crumbles

1 cup (195 g) cubed cheddar cheese

1 tbsp (18 g) kosher salt

1 tbsp plus 1½ tsp (19 g) granulated sugar

1 tbsp plus 1¼ tsp (17 g) active dry or instant yeast

Nonstick cooking spray

Cornmeal

⅓ cup (80 ml) melted butter, divided

In a large mixing bowl, stir together the flour, water, sausage, cheese, salt, sugar, and yeast with a sturdy spoon or dough whisk until the mixture is evenly moist with no dry pockets. The dough will be shaggy and very sticky. Spray a piece of plastic wrap with nonstick cooking spray and lay it loosely over the mixing bowl. Place the bowl in a warm, draft-free place until the dough looks puffy and bubbly, and has risen to about double its original size, about an hour.

While the dough rises, spray two loaf pans with nonstick cooking spray and sprinkle in a fistful of cornmeal. Tilt the pans, tapping gently, until the cornmeal coats the sides and bottoms of the pans, tapping out any excess cornmeal.

Use oil or nonstick cooking spray to generously grease your hands, and divide the dough between the two prepared pans. The pans should be no more than halfway full. If needed, prepare one more loaf pan to hold any excess dough.

Cover the pans loosely with oiled plastic wrap and let the dough rise in a warm, draft-free place until it is once again bubbly and puffy looking and just peeking above the edges of the pans, about 30 minutes. While the dough is rising, preheat the oven to 350°F (177°C).

Place the pans on the center rack in the oven and bake for 30 minutes. After 30 minutes, brush the surface of the bread generously with about half of the melted butter, then return the pans to the oven and bake 10 more minutes.

Immediately turn the loaves onto a cooling rack and brush all of the surfaces generously with the remaining melted butter. Cool completely before slicing or the texture will be compromised.

NOTES: Because this bread contains sausage, it must be stored in the refrigerator. This is best eaten within 4 days. If you'd like to store it longer, this bread is a good candidate for freezing. See freezing and defrosting instructions (page 177) for best results.

ENGLISH MUFFINS

If your fancy runs to classic English muffins, you can use any of the three English muffin bread recipes (pages 76, 79, and 80) in the book to make some spectacular ones. And English muffin rings are optional, but make your muffins more uniform in size and higher in rise.

Yield: 16 English muffins

Nonstick cooking spray

Cornmeal or semolina

1 risen batch of any English muffin bread dough (pages 76, 79, and 80)

Place two griddles on a cold stovetop. If your griddles are not nonstick or well seasoned, spray nonstick cooking spray first, then sprinkle both with a handful of cornmeal or semolina. If using, spray the insides of the English muffin rings with nonstick cooking spray and sprinkle cornmeal or semolina on the insides of the rings. Arrange eight rings on each griddle.

Use oil or nonstick cooking spray to generously grease your hands and divide the dough into sixteen equal pieces. Shape each piece into a smooth(ish) ball, then place in one of the prepared rings on the cold griddle. If you are not using rings, gently flatten the dough balls until they are an even ½ to ¾ inch (13 to 20 mm) thick. Use your fingers to gently flatten the discs of dough a bit, sprinkle the tops again with cornmeal or semolina, then cover the pans loosely with oiled plastic wrap and let rise for 20 to 25 minutes, or until beginning to look just a little puffy again.

Remove the plastic wrap and turn the heat to low under the griddles. Allow them to cook for about 7 minutes before flipping carefully. If you are using rings, it is okay if the rings slide off at this point. Cook for 4 to 8 more minutes, or until the English muffins are golden brown on both sides and the interior is 200°F (93°C) on an instant read thermometer.

Transfer to a cooling rack and allow them to cool completely before splitting with a fork or knife.

NOTES: Keep in mind that using the sausage and cheese dough will mean you need to store the finished muffins in the refrigerator or freezer.

As with all of the English Muffin Dough recipes, this one is particularly well suited to being frozen for longer storage. Please use the instructions for freezing and defrosting (page 177) for the best results.

If you'd like to maximize the "peaks and valleys" texture of your English muffins, use a fork to split them. To do this, insert a fork at three different places along the center line of the edge of your muffin, then pry it open.

SOFT PRETZEL DOUGH:

How to Win at Snacking

My kids like to play a game called "Keep One." In this game they choose only one item in an entire category of things to keep hypothetically. For instance, if I had to "keep one snack food," it would definitely be soft pretzels. They are the one food I categorically cannot refuse. I'll even eat the lousy ones at ballparks and movie theaters.

. . . But friends, homemade soft pretzels are in a category all by themselves. My recipe is the measure by which I judge all other soft pretzels. They're just the right amount of chewy with a deep, mahogany brown crust, and can be topped with classic coarse pretzel salt, garlic butter, cinnamon sugar, or everything bagel topping, just to name a few. Or you could top your pretzel with some of your favorite flavors in the Pepperoni Soft Pretzels (page 92) or Buffalo Chicken Soft Pretzels (page 95).

Here's the best part; they're all made with just one kind of dough. It seems almost like cheating to get that many possibilities from one little batch of dough, but learning that recipe is all you really need in order to make all of those treats, along with Pretzel Bread (page 89)—or shape into rolls or sliders, too!

While making a classic pretzel twist shape is fun, I more often make pretzel rods because it saves time and is easier to slather them with yellow mustard or beer cheese or whatever you like on your pretzels. Pssst. The right answer here is yellow mustard.

I find that whether I'm making soft pretzels, pretzel bread, or pretzel rolls of any size, the finished product is almost infinitely easier to remove from a pan that was lined with a silicone baking mat. The next best choice is a very generously oiled piece of parchment, but I still experience some sticking with that. If you opt for a plain pan, grease it very generously indeed and have a thin, flexible spatula that you can slide under the pretzels to help free them, but give them a few minutes to cool to avoid squishing them.

A word to the wise: soft pretzels, when untopped, can be frozen and reheated well. Pretzels need to be frozen and defrosted a little differently than most breads, so use these instructions instead of the ones that appear on page 177. A pretzel that has been topped with anything at all before freezing will suffer a bit texturally and visually when you thaw it. If you'd like to make a big batch of pretzels to stash for last-minute soft pretzel emergencies, bake them naked (the pretzels, not you), cool, freeze on the pans, and then wrap each one in foil before transferring to zipper-top freezer bags. When you'd like to eat them, take the desired number of pretzels from the freezer and place—still in their foil—on a parchment-lined pan. Open the foil, mist with water from a spray bottle, and sprinkle with pretzel salt before re-closing the foil. Place in a cold oven and set the heat for 250°F (130°C). When the oven reaches the proper temperature, cook for another 10 minutes and your pretzels should be hot and just as good as when they were new.

BUTTERY SOFT PRETZELS

While my kids play "Keep One" I grew up playing "Desert Island," and when asked which one food I'd eat on a desert island, my answer was always "soft pretzels." I'm not sure how I planned to manage whipping up soft pretzels on a desert island, but darn it, I was immovable. Soft pretzels are, to my mind, the ultimate snack. But if you serve them with a wedge of cheese, some carved ham, a couple of pickles, and a nice salad, I'd call it an incredible meal.

Have a look at the notes for some delicious variations on the soft pretzel theme including garlic butter, everything bagel, and cinnamon sugar. Don't be put off by the length of the instructions here—that is all due to the fact that I've included three different methods of shaping the pretzels so you can pick which one you like best!

Yield: 12 traditional pretzels, 16 pretzel rods, or a bunch of pretzel bites

PRETZEL DOUGH

4 cups (1 lb, 1 oz [482 g], by weight) bread flour

1 tbsp (13 g) sugar

1¼ tsp (8 g) kosher salt

2 tsp (8 g) active dry or instant yeast

1 cup (240 ml) whole milk

½ cup (120 ml) hot tap water

In a large mixing bowl or the bowl of a stand mixer, whisk together the flour, sugar, salt, and yeast. Set the whisk aside and switch to a sturdy wooden spoon. Stir in the milk and tap water until a soft dough forms. Knead the dough by hand or by stand mixer fitted with a dough hook for 5 to 8 minutes, or until you have a fairly slack, a little tacky and soft, smooth dough. Place the dough in a clean bowl, cover with a damp tea towel, and set aside to rise in a warm, draft-free place until nearly doubled in bulk and puffy, about an hour or so.

Line two half sheet pans with silicone baking mats. Set them aside.

TO MAKE A TRADITIONAL PRETZEL SHAPE

Use a bench knife to cut the dough into twelve equal pieces. Roll each piece like play-doh until you have a snake of dough about the circumference of your index finger.

Lay the snake of dough in a U-shape. Twist the two ends together twice, keeping the base of the "U" open, then fold the twisted ends down onto the base of the "U" and gently press in place.

Transfer the pretzels onto the lined baking sheets, being sure to leave generous amounts of room between them. They will expand both as they rise and again as they boil and bake. When you have dealt with all the dough, cover the pans with tea towels and let the pretzels rise in a warm, draft-free place until puffy looking, about 20 minutes.

TO MAKE EASIER PRETZEL RODS

Use a bench knife to cut the dough into sixteen equal pieces. Roll each piece like play-doh until you have a snake of dough about the circumference of your index finger. Transfer the pretzels onto the lined baking sheets, being sure to leave generous amounts of room between them. They will expand both as they rise and again as they boil and bake. When you have dealt with all the dough, cover the pans with tea towels and let the pretzels rise in a warm, draft-free place until puffy looking, about 20 minutes.

(continued)

PRETZEL BOIL

2 quarts (1.89 L) water

2 tbsp (28 g) baking soda

TOPPING

1 egg white, whisked until frothy

Pretzel salt or coarse kosher salt

6 tbsp (90 ml) melted butter

TO MAKE PRETZEL BITES

Turn the dough out and use a bench knife to cut the dough into four pieces. Keep three pieces covered with a tea towel while working with the first. Roll the piece like play-doh until you have a snake of dough about the circumference of two thumbs squashed together. Use your bench knife to cut 1-inch (3-cm) pieces from the doh snake. Transfer the dough pieces onto the lined baking sheets, being sure to leave generous amounts of room between pieces and rows. They will expand both as they rise and again as they boil and bake. When you have dealt with all the dough, cover the pans with tea towels and let the pretzels rise in a warm, draft-free place until puffy looking, about 20 minutes.

TO BOIL AND BAKE THE PRETZELS

Preheat the oven to 400°F (200°C).

Bring the water to a boil in a stainless steel or other nonreactive pan. When the water boils, add the baking soda. Gently lift the pretzel dough pieces one at a time into the boiling water.

You can boil more than one pretzel at a time, but be sure not to crowd the pan as they will expand as they boil. Let simmer for about 45 seconds, flip the pieces and simmer for another 45 seconds to 1 minute for pretzel bites, or 1 minute per side for pretzel rods or traditional pretzel shapes. Use a slotted spoon to drain and return each piece to its place on the sheet pan. Continue until all the pieces have been boiled and returned to the pan.

Brush all pieces of dough with the frothy egg white and sprinkle with coarse salt. Place pans in the oven and bake until golden brown—at least 10 minutes for bites, or at least 20 minutes for rods or traditional pretzel shapes—or you can bake a little longer until they are deep brown. It's up to you!

Brush the baked pretzels generously with melted butter while they're still hot, then transfer to a cooling rack if you're not eating them immediately.

NOTES: Turn your pretzels into garlic butter pretzels by whisking ¼ teaspoon of granulated garlic or 1 pressed or minced clove of garlic into the melted butter before brushing the finished pretzels.

For a little variety, you can swap out the pretzel salt for Everything Bagel Topping (page 172), sesame seeds, poppy seeds, or even cinnamon sugar.

Store leftover pretzels in a loosely cinched paper bag at room temperature. You can refresh them by misting with a little water from a spray bottle and wrapping in foil before sliding into a 250°F (130°C) oven for 15 minutes or until heated through.

For instructions on freezing and defrosting homemade soft pretzels, see the introduction to this chapter (page 85) for best results.

PRETZEL BREAD (WITH SLIDERS VARIATION)

Whether you make one perfect loaf of Pretzel Bread, sandwich-size pretzel rolls, or three-bite slider rolls, you will love this lovely, tempting, chewy yet tender, deep, dark brown bread.

Yield: 1 large loaf,
8 generous sandwich-size rolls,
or 12 slider rolls

PRETZEL DOUGH

4 cups (1 lb, 1 oz [482 g], by weight) bread flour

1 tbsp (13 g) sugar

1¼ tsp (8 g) kosher salt

2 tsp (8 g) active dry or instant yeast

1 cup (240 ml) whole milk

½ cup (120 ml) hot tap water

In a large mixing bowl or the bowl of a stand mixer, whisk together the flour, sugar, salt, and yeast. Set the whisk aside and switch to a sturdy wooden spoon. Stir in the milk and tap water until a soft dough forms. Knead the dough by hand or by stand mixer fitted with a dough hook for 5 to 8 minutes, or until you have a fairly slack, a little tacky and soft, smooth dough. Place the dough in a clean bowl, cover with a damp tea towel, and set aside to rise in a warm, draft-free place until nearly doubled in bulk and puffy, about an hour or so.

Line a half sheet pan with a silicone baking mat. Set it aside.

Turn the dough out onto the counter. Preheat the oven to 400°F (200°C).

FOR ONE LOAF OF BREAD

Lift the dough. Gently pull the edges of the dough down and tuck under. Turn the dough one-quarter turn and repeat. Do this until you've formed a cohesive round. Place the round on the clean surface and use your hands to gently turn and tighten the dough down over the surface. Place on the prepared pan, cover with a clean tea towel, and allow the dough to rise while the oven preheats.

FOR SANDWICH ROLLS

Divide the dough into eight equal pieces. Working with one piece at a time, form the dough into a ball, then cup your hand around the outside of the ball and roll clockwise until the top of the roll is perfectly smooth and the dough is tensely stretched over the top.

Transfer the dough balls onto the lined baking sheet, two to a row. They will expand both as they rise and again as they boil and bake. When you have dealt with all the dough, cover the pan with a tea towel and let the dough rise in a warm, draft-free place until puffy looking, about 20 minutes.

FOR SLIDER ROLLS

Divide the dough in twelve equal pieces. Working with one piece at a time, form the dough into a ball, then cup your hand around the outside of the ball and roll clockwise until the top of the roll is perfectly smooth and the dough is tensely stretched over the top.

Transfer the dough balls onto the lined baking sheet, three to a row. They will expand both as they rise and again as they boil and bake. When you have dealt with all the dough, cover the pan with a tea towel and let the dough rise in a warm, draft-free place until puffy looking, about 20 minutes.

(continued)

PRETZEL BREAD (WITH SLIDERS VARIATION) (CONT.)

PRETZEL BOIL

2 quarts (1.89 L) water

2 tbsp (28 g) baking soda

TOPPING

1 egg white, whisked until frothy

Pretzel salt or coarse kosher salt

TO BOIL AND BAKE THE BREAD

Preheat the oven to 400°F (200°C).

Bring the water to a gentle boil in a stainless steel or other nonreactive pan. When the water boils, add the baking soda. Gently lift the dough (one piece at a time, if making rolls or sliders) into the water.

If making the rolls or sliders, you can boil more than one at a time, but be sure not to crowd the pan as they will expand as they boil. Let simmer for 3 minutes per side for the loaf of bread, 1 minute per side for the rolls, or 45 seconds per side for the sliders. Use a slotted spoon to drain and return each piece to its place on the sheet pan. Continue until all pieces have been boiled and returned to the sheet pan.

Brush all the pieces of dough with the frothy egg white, then use a sharp knife to make three ¼-inch (6-mm)-deep slashes in the loaf, two per roll, or a small "X" per slider. Sprinkle lightly with coarse salt. Place the pans in the oven and bake at least 15 minutes for sliders, at least 20 minutes for rolls, or at least 35 minutes for a large loaf, but you can bake a little longer until they are deep brown for a chewier crust.

As soon as the sliders, rolls, or bread are done baking, transfer to a cooling rack to cool completely before slicing. Store leftovers at room temperature in a loosely cinched paper bag.

NOTE: For instructions on freezing and defrosting homemade soft pretzels, see the introduction to this chapter (page 85) for best results.

PEPPERONI SOFT PRETZELS

You may have seen—and if you're like me, bought—tempting pepperoni pizza pretzels at pretzel vendors at the mall or airport. These are, to put it succinctly, pretty much the best things ever. They're the happy marriage of two of my all-time favorite foods: pizza and soft pretzels. Serve them warm or at room temperature with a bowl of warm marinara sauce for dipping.

Yield: 10 traditional pretzel shapes or 12 pretzel rods

1 batch of risen Buttery Soft Pretzels dough (page 86)

2½ cups (220 g) shredded mozzarella cheese

50 to 60 slices of pepperoni

1 cup (80 g) grated Parmesan cheese

Sun-Dried Tomato Pesto (page 174) or marinara sauce, for serving (optional)

Preheat the oven to 400°F (200°C). Line two half sheet pans with silicone baking mats.

Shape, rise, and boil the pretzel dough according to the instructions found in the Buttery Soft Pretzels (page 86) recipe. Bake for 10 minutes, or until the pretzels have started to set and are darkening slightly.

Remove the pans from the oven and sprinkle ¼ cup (22 g) of shredded mozzarella evenly over each pretzel. Arrange five to six slices of pepperoni over each pretzel. Bake for another 10 to 15 minutes or until the cheese is melted and the pepperoni are starting to brown and crisp up in places. Scatter the Parmesan cheese evenly over the hot pretzels, then transfer the pretzels to a cooling rack for 5 minutes before serving warm with a bowl of Sun-Dried Tomato Pesto or your favorite pizza sauce, warmed.

NOTE: For instructions on freezing and defrosting homemade soft pretzels, see the introduction to this chapter (page 85) for best results, with one small difference: You will not need to mist this pretzel with water before re-wrapping with foil and reheating.

BUFFALO CHICKEN SOFT PRETZELS

I live near Buffalo, New York, and we take our Buffalo chicken seriously. Fun fact: we don't use the names "Buffalo wings" or "Buffalo sauce," we call them "wings" and "wing sauce" and everyone knows what we mean. But back to these pretzels. We're talking about our creamy, cheesy, spicy Buffalo Chicken Spread (page 175) packed onto chewy, soft pretzels baked until bubbly and hot. These are a little messy—like good wings always are—and so worth it.

Yield: 12 pretzels

1 batch of risen Buttery Soft Pretzels dough (page 86)

3 cups (720 ml) Buffalo Chicken Spread (page 175)

Bleu cheese dressing or Buffalo sauce for dip (optional)

Preheat the oven to 400°F (200°C). Line two half sheet pans with silicone baking mats.

Shape into the traditional pretzel shape, rise, and boil the pretzel dough according to the instructions found in the Buttery Soft Pretzels (page 86) recipe. Bake for 10 minutes, or until the pretzels have started to set and are darkening slightly.

Remove the pans from the oven and mound ⅓ cup (80 ml) of Buffalo Chicken Spread on each pretzel. Bake for another 10 to 15 minutes, or until the Buffalo Chicken Spread is bubbly and beginning to brown at the edges. Transfer the pretzels to a cooling rack for 5 minutes before serving warm with bleu cheese dressing or Buffalo sauce for dip, if desired.

NOTE: These pretzels are not suitable for freezing, but they reheat quite nicely when wrapped in foil and placed in a preheated 350°F (177°C) oven for about 20 minutes.

PRETZEL-WRAPPED LITTLE SMOKED SAUSAGES

I first tasted a version of this recipe at an Amish pretzel stand at an indoor farmers' market in Harrisburg, Pennsylvania, where several young Amish women were making these by the thousands.
I did not eat them by the thousands, but in the intervening years, I may have come close. These are a tradition for us during the Super Bowl and other festive occasions. We never have leftovers even when I double this recipe.

Yield: 4 dozen

1 batch risen Buttery Soft Pretzels dough (page 86)

ADDITIONAL INGREDIENTS

2 (14-oz [397-g]) packages cocktail-size smoked sausages

1 egg white whisked together with 1 tbsp (15 ml) cool water until frothy

Coarse pretzel salt

3 tbsp (45 ml) melted butter

Grainy mustard or horseradish sauce, for serving

FOR THE PRETZEL BOIL

2 quarts (1.89 L) water

2 tbsp (28 g) baking soda

Line two half sheet pans with silicone baking mats. Set aside.

Turn the risen dough out onto a clean, unfloured counter. Use a bench knife or dough scraper to cut off a piece of dough about the size of a ping pong ball. Cover the rest of the dough with a clean towel to keep it from drying.

Squash the piece of dough, then roll the piece of dough back and forth, gently moving your hands away from each other. Continue rolling the dough until it forms a long cord with a diameter of about ½ inch (13 mm).

Hold the end of the dough cord against the end of a cocktail sausage with one hand. Wind the dough around the sausage from end to end. Use a bench knife or spatula to cut off any extra cord. Pinch the loose ends of the cord into the dough coil. Place, pinched-side down, on the prepared pans. Repeat with the rest of the dough. Let rise, uncovered, for 20 minutes.

TO BOIL AND BAKE THE PRETZEL-WRAPPED SAUSAGES

While the pretzel dough is rising, preheat the oven to 400°F (200°C) and bring the water to a boil in a large pot. Add the baking soda to the boiling water. Carefully lower the wrapped sausages into the boiling water with your fingers. Do not overcrowd the pan. Simmer for about 1 minute, flipping over about 30 seconds in if they don't flip themselves. Use a slotted spoon to lift each piece from the water and return to the sheet pans.

Brush with the egg wash and sprinkle lightly with the coarse salt. Bake the trays for 16 minutes each, or until the pretzels are a glossy golden brown. Remove from the oven. Brush the finished pretzels with melted butter and cool for 5 minutes before transferring the pretzel sausages to a serving platter. Serve with grainy mustard or horseradish sauce.

BAGEL DOUGH:
No NYC Visit Required

A fresh homemade bagel is one of life's greatest pleasures. If you live in New York City or Montreal, you can't swing a brick of cream cheese without finding a great bagel shop. The rest of the continent isn't always so fortunate, and if you've never made your own bagels, you're in for a real treat. Your homemade bagels will far surpass any frozen bagel or bagged bagel you can get at most grocery stores.

Bagels are much easier to make than you might think and you have the option of making any of these bagel varieties into bagel sticks instead of a traditional hole-in-the-middle type. The bagel sticks are faster to shape and are great for sandwiches.

There are three basic bagel recipes in this chapter: plain, cinnamon raisin, and pumpernickel. You can turn the Plain Bagels and Bagel Sticks (page 100) base recipe into almost anything: onion, garlic, salt, sesame, poppy seed, cheese, jalapeño cheddar, or cinnamon sugar bagels, just to name a few. The plain bagel dough is so versatile, it can really hold up to just about any treatment you give it, whether savory or sweet.

The Pumpernickel Bagels and Bagel Sticks (page 103) base can be made into my all-time favorite bagel: a pumpernickel everything bagel, a.k.a. Black Russian Bagels. If you live in western New York you may be familiar with this variety of bagel sold freshly baked at the region's most popular grocery store, and now you can make them for yourself.

But bagel dough isn't just about the bagels, whether round or stick shaped . . . You can use the plain or pumpernickel bagel base to create the incredible Classic Onion Poppy Seed Bialys (page 107). These are bagel dough bases with a little well in place of the usual hole, topped with chopped onion, poppy seeds, and black pepper filling before being baked. The result is an irresistibly chewy roll with tender, flavorful onion and poppy seed filling. Eat them fresh from the oven when they're still warm from the oven, or wait until they've cooled and split them in half to use as a sandwich roll that is second to none.

The plain bagel base makes the most eminently snackable Pizza Bialys (page 108), too. These Pizza Bialys are built with no hole, much like the Classic Bialys, but the little indentation holds a dollop of garlicky pizza sauce and olive oil covered with a thick cap of pepperoni and melted mozzarella that browns around the edges. These are the happy marriage of bagels and pepperoni and are the most requested meal or snack by my children's friends for sleepovers. Everyone loves Pizza Bialys!

PLAIN BAGELS AND BAGEL STICKS (WITH TOPPING VARIATIONS)

Chewy, substantial, and magically delicious, homemade bagels are worlds better than any frozen bagel and most grocery store bagels, too. The plain bagel dough makes terrific "plain" bagels, but is also a canvas for numerous savory toppings.

Yield: 8 bagels

DOUGH

4½ cups (1 lb, 3.125 oz [570 g], by weight) bread flour

1 tbsp (13 g) sugar

1 tbsp (12 g) active dry or instant yeast

2 tsp (12 g) kosher salt

1¼ cups plus 2 tbsp (330 ml) warm water

BAGEL BOIL

2 quarts (1.89 L) water

3 tbsp (45 ml) mild honey

GLAZE

1 egg white beaten with 1 tbsp (15 ml) of water, whisked until frothy

In a mixing bowl or the bowl of a stand mixer, use a sturdy spoon to stir together the flour, sugar, yeast, and salt. Add the water and stir until a dry, shaggy dough starts to form. You can use a stand mixer to make the dough more cohesive, but make sure this is on a low speed to avoid burning out the motor. Turn the dough out and knead until smooth, 8 to 10 minutes. The dough will be quite stiff and sturdy, but should lose any dry appearance as you knead it. Form a neat round with the dough and place it in a clean bowl. Cover the bowl with a towel or shower cap and place in a warm, draft-free place to rise until doubled in bulk, 1 hour to 1½ hours.

Line two half sheet pans with silicone baking mats or parchment paper. Preheat the oven to 425°F (220°C). Combine the water and honey in a large skillet and bring to a gentle boil.

Divide the dough into eight equal pieces.

TO FORM BAGEL STICKS

Roll each piece of dough into a rod that is about 8 inches (20 cm) long. Arrange on the prepared pans, leaving 3 inches (8 cm) of space between each bagel stick. Cover loosely with plastic wrap or towels and allow the dough to rise for 20 minutes.

TO FORM TRADITIONAL BAGELS

Roll each piece of dough into a tight ball and arrange with 3 inches (8 cm) of space between the balls. Cover loosely with plastic wrap or towels and allow the dough to rise for 20 minutes.

Insert two fingers straight down into the center of one dough ball until you reach the pan. Use those fingers to lift the dough and to gently widen the hole in the center to about 2 inches (5 cm). Repeat this process with the other balls of dough.

TO BOIL AND BAKE THE BAGELS

Lower the raw bagels carefully into the gently boiling water, two to four at a time, depending on how much room you have in the skillet. Take care not to overcrowd the pan as they will expand a little as they boil. Boil the bagels for 1 minute on each side, then use a fish spatula or slotted spoon to lift and drain each bagel and return it to the sheet pan. Brush the boiled bagels with the egg wash, then top as desired (see next page). Bake for 20 to 25 minutes, or until a deep golden brown. Let the bagels rest on the pan for 10 minutes before transferring to a cooling rack to cool completely before slicing.

BAGEL TOPPINGS

The possibilities for topping these bagels are numerous. You can, of course, leave them with just the egg glaze, but try one or more of the following combinations just after brushing with the glaze and before baking, too!

- **Everything Bagels:** sprinkle each bagel with 1 to 2 teaspoons of Everything Bagel Topping (page 172)

- **Onion or Garlic Bagels:** sprinkle each bagel with ½ teaspoon of dehydrated garlic or onion flakes.

- **Asiago Garlic Bagels:** Toss together 1 cup (113 g) shredded Asiago and 1 minced clove of garlic. Sprinkle 2 tablespoons (14 g) of the mixture over each bagel.

- **Jalapeño Cheddar Bagels:** Top each bagel with 2 tablespoons (14 g) of shredded cheddar cheese and two to three thin slices of fresh jalapeño pepper.

NOTE: These are best kept loosely wrapped in a towel or parchment paper, or stored in a paper bag with the top cinched and folded down a couple of times.

PUMPERNICKEL BAGELS AND BAGEL STICKS (WITH BLACK RUSSIAN VARIATION)

Deep, dark, and unmistakably pumpernickel rye, this home version is lighter in texture than your average pumpernickel but still chewy and hearty like a great bagel should be. When they're topped with Everything Bagel Topping (page 172), these transform into my rendition of our favorite bagel shop variety: the Black Russian Bagel; also known as Pumpernickel Everything Bagels. These are delicious.

Yield: 8 bagels

DOUGH

4½ cups (1 lb, 3.125 oz [570 g], by weight) bread flour

⅓ cup plus 1 tbsp (51 g) Pumpernickel Bread Base (see page 172)

2 tsp (12 g) kosher salt

1 tbsp (14 g) brown sugar

1 tbsp (12 g) instant or active dry yeast

1¼ cups plus 2 tbsp (330 ml) lukewarm water

BAGEL BOIL

2 quarts (1.89 L) water

2 tbsp (28 g) brown sugar

TOPPING

1 egg white beaten with 1 tbsp (15 ml) water, whisked until frothy

⅓ cup (55 g) Everything Bagel Topping (page 172) for Black Russian Bagels

NOTE: These are best kept loosely wrapped in a towel or parchment paper, or stored in a paper bag with the top cinched and folded down a couple of times.

Whisk the flour, Pumpernickel Bread Base, salt, brown sugar, and yeast together in a large mixing bowl or the bowl of a stand mixer until even in color. Switch to a sturdy spoon, pour in the water, and stir until a shaggy dough forms. Knead by hand or machine for 5 to 10 minutes, or until a smooth dough forms. Form a neat ball with the dough, and place the dough in a clean bowl. Cover with a clean tea towel and let rise until doubled in bulk, 1 to 1½ hours.

Line two half sheet pans with silicone baking mats or parchment paper. Preheat the oven to 425°F (220°C). Combine the water and brown sugar in a large skillet and bring to a gentle boil.

Divide the dough into eight equal pieces.

TO FORM BAGEL STICKS

Roll each piece of dough into a rod that is about 8 inches (20 cm) long. Arrange on the prepared pans, leaving 3 inches (8 cm) of space between each bagel stick. Cover loosely with plastic wrap or towels and allow the dough to rise for 20 minutes.

TO FORM TRADITIONAL BAGELS

Roll each piece of dough into a tight ball and arrange with 3 inches (8 cm) of space between the balls. Cover loosely with plastic wrap or towels and allow the dough to rise for 20 minutes.

Insert two fingers straight down into the center of one dough ball until you reach the pan. Use those fingers to lift the dough and to gently widen the hole in the center to about 2 inches (5 cm). Repeat this process with the other balls of dough.

TO BOIL AND BAKE THE BAGELS

Lower the raw bagels carefully into the gently boiling water, two to four at a time, depending on how much room you have in the skillet. Take care not to overcrowd the pan as they will expand a little as they boil. Boil the bagels for 1 minute on each side, then use a fish spatula or slotted spoon to lift and drain each bagel and return it to the sheet pan. Brush the boiled bagels with the egg wash, then sprinkle with Everything Bagel Topping, if desired. Bake for 20 to 25 minutes, or until the bagels are a glossy dark brown. Let the bagels rest on the pan for 10 minutes before transferring to a cooling rack to cool completely before slicing.

CINNAMON RAISIN BAGELS AND BAGEL STICKS

Cinnamon raisin bagels are a sweet standout in what I consider to be a category rightfully dominated by savory options. The process of kneading the dough over the cinnamon sugar helps create the characteristic swirls that make these bagels sweet both literally and figuratively.

Yield: 8 bagels

DOUGH

⅓ cup (66 g) sugar

1 tsp cinnamon

1 batch kneaded but unrisen plain bagel dough (page 100)

⅔ cup (95 g) raisins

BAGEL BOIL

2 quarts (1.89 L) water

3 tbsp (45 ml) mild honey

GLAZE

1 egg white beaten with 1 tbsp (15 ml) water, whisked until frothy

In a small mixing bowl, use a fork to combine the sugar and cinnamon until it is an even color. Pour it in a neat pile on a clean counter or a counter lined with a silicone baking mat. Place the kneaded dough on top of the pile of cinnamon sugar. Press the dough outward and pour the raisins on the dough. Fold the dough in half to encase the raisins and knead the dough over the cinnamon sugar for about 4 minutes. The cinnamon sugar will swirl into the dough and the raisins should be incorporated as you continue to knead. Form a neat round and place it in a clean bowl. Cover the bowl with a towel or shower cap and place it in a warm, draft-free place to rise until doubled in bulk, 1 to 1½ hours.

Line two half sheet pans with silicone baking mats or parchment paper. Preheat the oven to 425°F (220°C). Combine the water and honey in a large skillet and bring to a gentle boil. Divide the dough into eight equal pieces.

TO FORM BAGEL STICKS

Roll each piece of dough into a rod that is about 8 inches (20 cm) long. Arrange on the prepared pans, leaving 3 inches (8 cm) of space between each bagel stick. Cover loosely with plastic wrap or towels and allow the dough to rise for 20 minutes.

TO FORM TRADITIONAL BAGELS

Roll each piece of dough into a tight ball and arrange with 3 inches (8 cm) of space between the balls. Cover loosely with plastic wrap or towels and allow the dough to rise for 20 minutes.

Insert two fingers straight down into the center of one dough ball until you reach the pan. Use those fingers to lift the dough and to gently widen the hole in the center to about 2 inches (5 cm). Repeat this process with the other balls of dough.

TO BOIL AND BAKE THE BAGELS

Lower the raw bagels carefully into the gently boiling water, two to four at a time, depending on how much room you have in the skillet. Take care not to overcrowd the pan as they will expand a little as they boil. Boil the bagels for 1 minute on each side, then use a fish spatula or slotted spoon to lift and drain each bagel and return it to the sheet pan. Brush the bagels with the egg wash. Bake for 20 to 25 minutes, or until a deep golden brown. Let the bagels rest on the pan for 10 minutes before transferring to a cooling rack to cool completely before slicing.

CLASSIC ONION POPPY SEED BIALYS

Unless you frequent New York City bakeries, you may not have encountered these beautiful little breads, but you are going to want to make their acquaintance, because these cousins of the bagel are habit-forming. Where bagels have holes, bialys have deep indentations that traditionally hold a flavorful filling of onions, poppy seeds, black pepper, and a little oil. And unlike bagels, they're not boiled. They're slightly more substantial, and—no disrespect intended to my lifetime best beloved bagel—a little more grown up than bagels. You can eat them as is or split them for a sandwich roll that will be the envy of anyone watching you eat your lunch.

Yield: 8 generous-size bialys

1 batch risen plain bagel dough (page 100)

1 cup (160 g) chopped onion

1 tbsp (8 g) poppy seeds

1 tsp Garlic Olive Oil (page 173)

½ tsp kosher salt

¼ tsp black pepper

Line two half sheet pans with silicone baking mats or parchment paper.

Divide the dough into eight equal pieces. Roll each piece into a tight ball and place on the prepared baking sheets, leaving 3 inches (8 cm) of space between the balls. Flatten gently with your hands. Cover the dough loosely with plastic wrap or towels and let it rise in a warm, draft-free place for 30 minutes.

Preheat the oven to 425°F (220°C) while the dough rises and prepare the filling. Place the onions on a microwave-safe plate and microwave for 1½ minutes. Stir the onions and microwave for 1 more minute. Add the poppy seeds, oil, salt, and black pepper to the onions and stir to distribute. Set aside.

Use the pads of three fingers to press a well into the bialy dough. You should press down far enough to feel the pan beneath the dough, but not so far that you make a hole in it. Repeat this with the rest of the bialys. Divide the onion filling between the bialys, spooning it into the wells you created.

Bake the bialys for 20 to 25 minutes, rotating the pans from top to bottom and front to back midway through baking, or until the bialys are golden brown and set. Let them cool on the pans for 10 minutes before transferring to a rack to cool completely.

Bialys can be stored tightly wrapped at room temperature for up to 3 days.

PIZZA BIALYS

Did I call bialys grown up? I hereby take that back and present to you pizza bialys. There's not even a pretense of sophistication to these but boy are they good. These bialys have a dollop of pizza sauce in their wells and are covered by a generous cap of melted, browning cheese. If you're so inclined, feel free to top them with pepperoni slices.

Yield: 8 generous-size bialys

1 batch risen plain bagel dough (page 100)

½ cup (120 ml) pizza sauce

1 tbsp (15 ml) Garlic Olive Oil (page 173)

2 cups (170 g) shredded mozzarella

1 clove garlic, minced or pressed

24 slices pepperoni (optional)

Line two half sheet pans with silicone baking mats or parchment paper.

Divide the dough into eight equal pieces. Roll each piece into a tight ball and place on the prepared baking sheets, leaving 3 inches (8 cm) of space between the rolls. Flatten gently with your hands. Cover the dough loosely with plastic wrap or towels and let rise in a warm, draft-free place for 30 minutes.

Preheat the oven to 425°F (220°C) while the dough rises and prepare the filling. In a small bowl, stir together the pizza sauce and oil. In a second bowl, toss together the shredded mozzarella and the minced garlic.

Use the pads of three fingers to press a well into the bialy dough. You should press down far enough to feel the pan beneath the dough, but not so far that you make a hole in it. Repeat this with the rest of the bialys. Spoon about 1 tablespoon (15 ml) of the sauce into the wells you created, then about ¼ cup (22 g) of the garlic cheese over the top of each bialy. If you're using the pepperoni, arrange three slices on each bialy.

Bake the bialys for 20 to 25 minutes, rotating the pans from top to bottom and front to back midway through baking, or until the bialys are golden brown, and the cheese is bubbly and browning in areas. Let them cool on the pans for 10 minutes before transferring to a rack to cool completely. These are great eaten warm or at room temperature.

Pizza bialys can be stored tightly wrapped in the refrigerator up to 3 days. To reheat, wrap in foil and place in a 250°F (130°C) oven for 20 minutes.

ENRICHED EGG DOUGH:

Soft and Dreamy Bread

If you asked me which bread in this book reminds me most of my grandmother's bread, I would answer "enriched egg dough" with no hesitation. It's a rich, buttery, pillowy soft, white bread—just like the prized bread loaf that my grandpa loved best and my grandma made in super-human quantities.

Unlike the white bread found in most grocery stores, this one has character and body from the eggs, dairy, and butter it includes. It gets a little boost in color from the egg yolk so it's prettier than the average white bread and is pretty similar in texture, flavor, and color to a beautiful brioche.

That little extra body in the enriched egg dough in the Pillowy Soft Sandwich Bread (page 112) yields a bread that makes an amazing peanut butter and jelly sandwich, but can still hold up a pile of sandwich toppings. It's tender yet substantial.

The dough is also the perfect jumping off place to make the best Hamburger or Sandwich Rolls (page 115) I've ever eaten, if I do say so myself. Don't just count on me, though; ask my kids! If you should decide to gild the lily and toast or grill the split bun before topping it, you're going to be terribly pleased with yourself.

You can also use this dough for Miami Onion Rolls (page 119) a.k.a Onion Pockets. These addictive little rolls are made by letting enriched egg dough rise on top of some crisp-tender, cooked onions and poppy seeds. The dough is then patted out, rolled up, and cut to form little pockets of tender onions. These are a natural pairing with soups and stews, but also make great sandwich rolls when you split them like a burger bun. Good luck resisting these!

Don't stop there, though! Use enriched egg dough to whip up some delectable treats to satisfy the sweet tooth in your life, whether it's the caramel-like Fluffy Cinnamon Rolls with Cream Cheese Icing (page 116), bright and sunshiny Lemon Glazed Soft Swirl Bread (with Blueberry Variation) (page 120), Chai Spiced Monkey Bread (page 123), or Dark Chocolate Raspberry Swirl Bread (page 124) packed with dark chocolate chunks and swirls of real raspberry preserves.

PILLOWY SOFT SANDWICH BREAD

This old-fashioned bread is what white bread was originally intended to be: high-rising, pillowy, soft, and full of flavor. This bread is never bland and never, ever boring and is like a big hug from your sweet grandma; it's always welcome. The egg and butter added to it give it richness, body, and texture. It is equally delicious sliced for sandwiches, topped with butter and preserves, or toasted.

Yield: 2 loaves

DOUGH

4 cups (1 lb, 1 oz [482 g], by weight) bread flour

3 tbsp (11 g) plain instant mashed potato flakes, any brand

3 tbsp (38 g) granulated sugar

2 tsp (12 g) kosher salt

2 tsp (8 g) active dry or instant yeast

1¼ cups (300 ml) lukewarm milk

6 tbsp (84 g) unsalted butter, softened to room temperature

1 egg, beaten

Nonstick cooking spray

GLAZE

1 egg beaten with 1 tbsp (15 ml) water

In a large mixing bowl or the bowl of a stand mixer, whisk together the flour, instant potato flakes, sugar, salt, and yeast. Set the whisk aside and switch to a sturdy wooden spoon. Stir in the milk, butter, and egg until a shaggy dough forms. Knead the dough by hand or by stand mixer fitted with a dough hook for 8 to 10 minutes, or until you have a smooth and elastic dough. Place the dough in a clean bowl, cover with a damp tea towel, and set aside to rise in a warm, draft-free place until nearly doubled in bulk and puffy, about an hour or so.

Spritz two loaf pans lightly with nonstick cooking spray. Set them aside.

Turn the dough out onto the counter. Divide the dough into two equal pieces and gently pat each piece into a rectangle that is approximately 8 x 12 inches (20 x 30 cm). Starting at the short end, roll up each piece of dough tightly to form a log, tuck the ends underneath, and ease into a prepared loaf pan with the tucked sides down. Cover the pans with a towel and set aside in a warm, draft-free place until puffy, about 30 minutes to 1 hour.

Preheat the oven to 375°F (190°C) while the dough rises. Brush the loaves generously with the egg wash and bake for 35 to 40 minutes, or until the bread measures about 190°F (88°C) on an instant read thermometer. Transfer the bread from the bread pans to a cooling rack and allow to cool completely before slicing. Store tightly wrapped at room temperature for up to 1 week.

HAMBURGER OR SANDWICH ROLLS

If there is one thing that makes the burgers in our world, it's the bun, and this is the best of all time. All of the things that make this dough such a wonderful slicing bread also make it an incredible burger or sandwich roll. It is sturdy enough to stack high with burgers and all the toppings your heart can desire, and also soft enough to bite into when you've done that. Let's see an eight-to-the-package-bun manage that! See the Notes for instructions on making hot dog rolls or slider buns.

Yield: 12 generous-size rolls or hot dog buns, or 16 sliders

1 batch risen Pillowy Soft Sandwich Bread dough (page 112)

GLAZE

1 egg beaten with 1 tbsp (15 ml) water

TOPPINGS

Sesame seeds

Poppy seeds

Dehydrated onion flakes

Dehydrated garlic flakes

Line two half sheet pans with parchment paper or silicone baking mats and set them aside.

Divide the dough into twelve equal pieces and roll each piece into a tight ball. Place six on each prepared sheet pan, leaving 2 to 3 inches (5 to 8 cm) between each roll to allow for expansion during rising and baking. Slightly flatten the dough balls with your hands. Cover the dough with a towel and set in a warm, draft-free place to rise until puffy, about 30 minutes. Preheat the oven to 375°F (190°C) while the dough rises.

Brush the rolls with the egg wash and sprinkle with the desired toppings. Bake for 18 to 22 minutes, or until the rolls are a glossy, deep golden brown. Transfer to a rack to cool completely before slicing. Store tightly wrapped at room temperature for up to 2 days.

NOTES: For longer storage, see the instructions on freezing and defrosting (page 177) for best results.

To make sliders, cut the dough into sixteen pieces instead of twelve, shape, let rise, brush with the egg wash, and bake for 12 to 16 minutes, or until glossy and golden brown.

To make hot dog buns, divide the dough into twelve pieces and flatten, then roll into 6-inch (15-cm) rods. Space the rods 2 to 3 inches (5 to 8 cm) apart, then let rise, brush with the egg wash, and bake as instructed.

FLUFFY CINNAMON ROLLS WITH CREAM CHEESE ICING

There is nothing in the world that compares to a warm, fluffy cinnamon roll dripping with cream cheese icing. Everyone in the United States knows what a cinnamon roll looks and smells like, but my recipe is a particularly good version of the treat. The dough is so silky it practically rolls itself out, and it bakes up into the fluffiest, softest cinnamon rolls ever. These make my entire family so happy.

Yield: 12 generous-sized rolls

Nonstick cooking spray

½ cup (100 g) granulated sugar

1 tbsp (8 g) Chai Spice Blend (page 173)

½ cup (113 g) butter, super soft

1 batch risen Pillowy Soft Sandwich Bread dough (page 112)

FROSTING

6 oz (170 g) cream cheese, softened to room temperature

4 tbsp (56 g) butter, softened to room temperature

2 cups (220 g) powdered sugar

1 tbsp plus 1½ tsp (24 ml) pure vanilla, orange, or maple extract

Spray a 9 x 13-inch (23 x 33–cm) baking pan with nonstick cooking spray. Set aside.

In a small mixing bowl, use a fork to toss together the sugar and Chai Spice Blend. Use the same fork to start squishing the butter into the sugar mixture. When it is mostly incorporated, switch to a spatula to cream the mixture together.

Roll the dough out to a rectangle that is approximately 12 x 15 inches (30 x 38 cm). Spread the butter and sugar mixture evenly over the rectangle, leaving 1 inch (3 cm) of one long edge free of the mixture. Starting at the long edge that has butter, roll it up tightly, jelly-roll style. Pinch together the seams. Cut the roll of dough into twelve equal pieces. Arrange the pieces on the prepared pan in four rows of three. Cover the dough loosely with plastic wrap.

Preheat the oven to 375°F (190°C) while the dough rises. Remove the plastic wrap and bake for 25 minutes or until the center of the rolls measure 190°F (88°C) on an instant read thermometer. Cool completely.

While the rolls bake, use a hand mixer or sturdy spoon to mix the cream cheese and butter together until fluffy. Beat in the powdered sugar and extract until smooth, then spread over the cooled rolls. Store leftovers, tightly wrapped, at room temperature.

MIAMI ONION ROLLS

These rolls are utterly irresistible and that's just the truth. You've been warned. I find myself "taste testing" one of these tender rolls studded with onions and poppy seeds right when the pan comes out of the oven. Okay, I taste test two or three, but let's see you behave better when you're breathing in the tempting aroma of these glossy brown little onion pockets.

Yield: 12 rolls

1 cup (160 g) onion, ¼-inch (6-mm) dice

2 tsp (7 g) poppy seeds

1 batch kneaded but unrisen Pillowy Soft Sandwich Bread dough (page 112)

1 egg beaten with 1 tbsp (15 ml) water

Spread the onions on a microwave-safe plate and microwave for 1½ minutes. Stir the onions and microwave for 30 seconds. Spread the onions over the base and up along the inside of a medium-size mixing bowl, then sprinkle the poppy seeds evenly over the onions. Form the bread dough into a neat round and nestle it over the onions. Cover the bowl with a shower cap, plastic wrap or towel. Set the bowl in a warm, draft-free place until puffy and doubled in bulk, 1 to 1½ hours.

Line two half sheet pans with parchment paper or silicone baking mats.

Turn the dough out onto a clean counter. Pat or roll the dough out into a rectangle that is about 12 x 18 inches (30 x 46 cm). Fold both short ends of the dough in toward the center of the dough and then in half like a book. Roll this rectangle out to a square that is about 12 x 12 inches (30 x 30 cm). Use a bench knife or pizza cutter to cut this into four rows lengthwise and three rows widthwise to yield twelve equal rectangles. Transfer the rolls to the prepared pans, leaving 2 to 3 inches (5 to 8 cm) of space between the rolls to allow for expansion during rising and baking.

Preheat the oven to 375°F (190°C) while the dough rises. Brush the rolls generously with the egg wash and bake for 20 to 25 minutes, or until they measure about 190°F (88°C) on an instant read thermometer. Let the rolls rest on the pans for 5 minutes, then transfer to a cooling rack and allow to cool completely before slicing. Store tightly wrapped at room temperature for up to 4 days.

NOTE: These rolls are an excellent candidate for freezing. Follow the instructions on freezing and defrosting (page 177) for best results.

LEMON GLAZED SOFT SWIRL BREAD (WITH BLUEBERRY VARIATION)

One bite of this soft, brightly-lemony–flavored bread will have you singing, "Good day, sunshine!" A simple buttery and sweet lemon filling is swirled through bread topped with a lemon glaze. Delicious for eating as is, or toasting in a pan with a little butter, this is great with tea and coffee for a morning or afternoon pick-me-up. Be sure to read the notes for a quick and easy 1-ingredient way to turn this into a Lemon Glazed Soft Blueberry Swirl bread.

Yield: 2 loaves

FILLING

⅔ cup (132 g) granulated sugar

2 tbsp (16 g) all-purpose flour

Zest of 3 lemons

BREAD

Nonstick cooking spray or oil

1 batch risen Pillowy Soft Sandwich Bread dough (page 112)

1 egg beaten with 1 tbsp (15 ml) water as an egg wash

LEMON GLAZE

½ cup (55 g) powdered sugar

1 tbsp (15 ml) fresh lemon juice

¼ tsp vanilla extract

In a medium-size mixing bowl, use a fork to toss together the sugar, flour, and lemon zest. Lightly spray two loaf pans with nonstick cooking spray. Set aside.

Divide the dough into two equal pieces. Cover one with a towel. Roll or pat out one piece to a rectangle that is approximately 10 x 18 inches (25 x 46 cm). Brush the egg wash liberally over the rectangle, leaving one long edge free of egg wash 1 inch (3 cm) from the edge. Sprinkle half of the filling mixture over the loaf, stopping where the egg wash stops.

Starting at the long side that is egg washed, roll up the dough tightly. Pinch the seams and ends, then double the roll back so you have a tight oval double roll. Pinch the ends together again and tuck under before easing it into the loaf pan, with the tucked ends facing down. Repeat with the second piece of dough, more egg wash, and the remaining filling mixture. Cover the loaf pans with a towel and place in a warm, draft-free place to rise until the dough is puffy looking again and just rising above the top of the loaf pan, about 1 hour. Brush the dough with the remaining egg wash.

Preheat the oven to 375°F (190°C) while the dough rises. Bake the bread for 30 to 35 minutes or until it is a darker golden brown and reaches 190°F (88°C) on an instant read thermometer. Let the bread rest in the pan for 10 minutes before turning the bread out onto a cooling rack.

When the dough is barely warm to the touch, prepare the glaze by using a whisk to combine the powdered sugar, lemon juice, and vanilla extract until smooth. Use a pastry brush to brush all over the tops and sides of the loaves. Let them finish cooling completely before slicing.

NOTES: It is very easy to turn this luscious lemon loaf into a Lemon Glazed Soft Blueberry Swirl bread. After you've sprinkled the filling mixture over the egg wash, just sprinkle ⅓ cup (55 g) of dried blueberries over the top. Roll up, let it rise, bake, and glaze as instructed above.

If you think you can't eat both loaves of bread within 5 days, it freezes best unglazed. To eat one and freeze one, just halve the quantities of ingredients in the glaze. Let the unglazed loaf cool completely before wrapping in a double thickness of foil, then in plastic wrap, and freezing. See the instructions on freezing and defrosting bread (page 177) for the best results.

CHAI SPICED MONKEY BREAD

Monkey bread is the happy, pull-apart combination of hot, sticky caramel and tender bread pieces rolled in cinnamon sugar. It's pretty simple to make and pretty spectacular looking. An indulgent, silky butter caramel sauce forms around the bread as it bakes in a 10-cup (10-L) Bundt pan. When it's done baking, you place a plate on top of the pan and carefully flip it over; as you lift the pan, the caramel sauce pours over the top and down the sides of the bread. This is a surefire winner at any party, and can make any day seem like a special one.

Yield: 1 large loaf

Nonstick cooking spray

1 cup (200 g) granulated sugar

1 tbsp (8 g) Chai Spice Blend (page 173)

1 batch risen Pillowy Soft Sandwich Bread dough (page 112)

1 cup (225 g) butter

½ cup (110 g) brown sugar, packed

Spray a 10-cup (10-L) Bundt pan heavily with nonstick cooking spray. Set aside.

In a zipper-top bag, combine the granulated sugar and Chai Spice Blend. Close the bag and shake to combine.

Divide the dough into three pieces. Cover two with a towel. Roll out one piece into a rope that is about 1 inch (3 cm) in diameter. Cut crosswise into 1-inch (3-cm) pieces. Toss the pieces into the chai spice sugar mixture a few at a time, then transfer to the prepared Bundt pan. Repeat this with the remaining dough. Cover and let rise for 20 minutes.

Preheat the oven to 375°F (190°C) while the dough rises. While the oven preheats and the dough rises, add the butter, ½ cup (100 g) of the remaining chai spice sugar, and the brown sugar to a small saucepan over high heat, stirring as the butter melts. Bring just to a full boil, then immediately remove the caramel and pour over the risen dough.

Place the Bundt pan on a rimmed baking pan and bake the bread for 35 to 40 minutes or until it is a deep brown and reaches 190°F (88°C) on an instant read thermometer. Let the bread rest in the pan for 5 to 8 minutes before topping the pan with a rimmed plate or serving platter that extends beyond the edges of the Bundt pan. Holding the plate in place, carefully flip the pan and plate over together. Tap the Bundt pan a few times, then carefully lift it from the plate. The caramel should pour from the pan over the bread. Be careful because that caramel is *hot*! Serve warm or at room temperature.

DARK CHOCOLATE RASPBERRY SWIRL BREAD

What can I tell you about this bread? It's a rich, tender bread baked around a double swirl of raspberry preserves and chocolate pieces. It is decadent, delicious, and not at all hard on the eyes. A friend described this as being "great for lazy people. It's like if you spread jam and Nutella on bread, but all you have to do is cut a slice and eat it." This makes a great brunch loaf or accompaniment to your afternoon cup of tea or coffee.

Yield: 2 loaves

1 cup (320 g) raspberry preserves

2 tbsp (16 g) all-purpose flour

Nonstick cooking spray or oil

1 batch risen Pillowy Soft Sandwich Bread dough (page 112)

1 egg beaten with 1 tbsp (15 ml) water as an egg wash

⅔ cup (110 g) bittersweet or dark chocolate chunks or chips

In a small mixing bowl, use a fork or small whisk to loosen up the preserves. Sprinkle the flour over the top and blend until even.

Lightly spray two loaf pans with nonstick cooking spray. Set aside.

Divide the dough into two equal pieces. Cover one with a towel. Roll or pat out one piece to a rectangle that is approximately 8 x 18 inches (20 x 46 cm). Brush the egg wash liberally over the rectangle, leaving one long edge free of egg wash 1 inch (3 cm) from the edge. Spread half of the preserve mixture over the egg wash. Sprinkle half of the chocolate chunks or chips over the loaf, stopping where the preserves and egg wash stops.

Starting at the long side that has jam spread on it, roll up the dough tightly. Pinch the seams and ends, then double the roll back so you have a tight double roll oval. Pinch the ends together again and tuck under before easing it into the loaf pan, with the tucked ends facing down. Repeat with the second piece of dough, more egg wash, the remaining preserve mixture and the remaining chocolate. Cover the loaf pans with a towel and place in a warm, draft-free place to rise until the dough is puffy looking again and just rising above the top of the loaf pan, about 1 hour. Brush the dough with the egg wash.

Preheat the oven to 375°F (190°C) while the dough rises. Bake the bread for 40 minutes or until it is a darker golden brown and reaches 190°F (88°C) on an instant read thermometer. Let the bread rest in the pan for 10 minutes before turning the bread out onto a cooling rack.

NOTES: This is a great candidate for freezing and eating later. For the best results, see the instructions on freezing and defrosting bread (page 177).

If your preference is for milk or semi-sweet chocolate, feel free to substitute it for the dark or bittersweet chocolate in equal quantities.

Never Boring

OATMEAL
BREAD DOUGH

This is the shortest chapter in the book, with just three recipes, but oh what recipes those three are! This bread dough was one of the very first recipes that inspired me to write this book and I cannot wait for you to try it.

Oatmeal Bread is the stuff of happy memories for me. My beloved stepmom, Valerie, specialized in this oatmeal dough that seemed to be made in heaven. It was a brown loaf, topped with toasted oats, which had a soft, yet chewy, crumb that smelled like toasty nirvana as it baked. It required superhuman effort to allow it to cool completely before slicing. This, as my stepmom told me, was the purpose of two loaves. One loaf was to be allowed to cool completely for slicing and making sandwiches or toast later, while the second loaf was to keep us virtuous by being sacrificed to the insatiable urge to nibble while the first loaf cooled. There was no regret when we completely consumed the sacrificial loaf because we had the other loaf sitting there doing what it was supposed to be doing: setting up in the crumb to make a hearty and nutty-flavored slicing bread that we loved for roasted turkey or herbed cream cheese and cucumber sandwiches or thickly sliced for toast with homemade strawberry freezer jam and Nutella.

But as wonderful as that bread was, we were all even more excited when she turned half of the batch into what she called cheater pain au chocolat: a soft, brown, butter-brushed oat roll stuffed with an impossible number of melted chocolate chips. Just imagine coming in from a cold winter day to a plate full of Chocolate-Stuffed Oat Buns (page 132) and a tall cup of tea and you will get a glimpse into what made eating at Val's table so wonderful.

The dough is also the jumping off point for what I believe is the best Cinnamon Swirl Streusel-Topped Oat Bread (page 131) I can find; it is full of a raisin and cinnamon filling that is blitzed in the food processor until finely minced. This unusual treatment for the raisins makes a sweet bread redolent with cinnamon that even my raisin-haters love.

GRANDMA VAL'S OATMEAL SANDWICH BREAD

There will never be another bread as made-for-toast as Grandma Val's Oatmeal Sandwich Bread. Don't get me wrong, it is soft and sturdy when fresh, and it's hard to beat a piece of it warm with butter or Nutella on top, but toast is where this bread really shines. This nutty whole grain bread gets extra toothsomeness from oats in the dough and on the crust that take on extra deliciousness when toasted in a toaster or in a frying pan with a little butter. This will be one you find yourself doubling time and again because it's hard to keep it around.

Yield: 2 loaves

1¼ cups (100 g) quick oats, divided

1 cup (4.25 oz [120 g], by weight) whole wheat flour

⅓ cup (73 g) light brown sugar

1 tbsp (18 g) kosher salt

2 tbsp (28 g) butter

2 cups (480 ml) boiling water

1 tbsp (12 g) instant yeast

3½ cups (12.75 oz [362 g], by weight) all-purpose flour

Nonstick cooking spray

1 egg beaten with 1 tbsp (15 ml) water

In a heat-proof stainless steel or glass mixing bowl, or the bowl of a stand mixer, whisk together 1 cup (80 g) of the quick oats, the whole wheat flour, brown sugar, and salt. Cut the butter into several small pieces and scatter the butter over the top of the flour mixture. Pour the boiling water over it all and whisk until evenly combined and the butter is melted. Cover with plastic wrap and let it set at room temperature until it is lukewarm. Whisk one more time, then sprinkle the yeast over the surface of the warm oat mixture.

Use a sturdy spoon or spatula to work in the all-purpose flour until a shaggy dough forms. The dough will be tacky even when done, but should hold together. This is kneaded most easily in a stand mixer fitted with a dough hook, but can be kneaded by hand on a silicone baking mat or lightly floured counter. Form the dough into a neat mass and put it in a clean bowl.

Cover the bowl with a clean tea towel and let the dough rise in a warm, draft-free place until doubled in bulk, 35 to 45 minutes.

Spray two loaf pans with nonstick cooking spray. Divide the dough into two evenly sized pieces. Pat out and roll into a loaf-pan–size shape, then ease into the prepared pans. Brush with the egg wash, then sprinkle the remaining ¼ cup (20 g) of oats over the loaves. Cover and let the dough rise again until doubled once more, 30 to 40 minutes. Bake in a preheated 350°F (177°C) oven for 35 to 45 minutes, or until the loaf is set, deeply golden brown, and reaches at least 190°F (88°C) on an instant read thermometer.

CINNAMON SWIRL STREUSEL-TOPPED OAT BREAD

I have two kids who—under normal circumstances—won't touch raisins with a 10-foot pole. Those same kids inhale this bread that includes a herculean portion of raisins. How is this possible? It is because the raisins are ground with cinnamon and brown sugar and a wee bit of flour to form a sweet sandy mixture that melts into the most wonderfully moist cinnamon swirl with zero discernable raisins in it. Guys, it is not possible for me to oversell this bread. It sends people into raptures.

Yield: 2 loaves

Nonstick cooking spray

FILLING

⅔ cup (120 g) raisins

½ cup (110 g) brown sugar

¼ cup (50 g) granulated sugar

4 tsp (11 g) all-purpose flour

BREAD

1 batch risen Grandma Val's Oatmeal Sandwich Bread dough (page 128)

1 large egg beaten with 1 tbsp (15 ml) water until smooth

STREUSEL

½ cup (63 g) all-purpose flour

¼ cup (50 g) granulated sugar

2 tbsp (10 g) quick oats

½ tsp ground cinnamon

¼ cup (56 g) cold butter

Spray two loaf pans with nonstick cooking spray.

Add the raisins, brown sugar, granulated sugar, and flour to the bowl of a food processor fitted with a metal blade. Pulse until the raisins have been ground and the mixture resembles wet, clumpy sand. Set aside.

Divide the dough in half. Cover one half of the dough with a towel to keep it from drying out. Roll the other half out to a rectangle that is about 8 x 16 inches (20 x 41 cm). Brush the rectangle generously with the egg wash, then sprinkle half of the raisin filling over the egg.

On the long side of the rectangle, begin rolling the dough up log-roll style. Keep the roll tight, stretching it slightly as you roll it up. Making a tight roll helps eliminate air pockets in the swirl. Pinch the seams closed, then double the log of dough halfway back on itself so you have what looks like two logs side by side. Pinch the ends to form an oval, then tuck the pinched ends under, and ease it into a prepared pan. Repeat with the other half of the dough, egg wash, and remaining raisin filling. Cover with a towel and let the dough rise for about an hour, or until it has just crested above the edge of the pan.

While the dough is rising in the pans, preheat the oven to 350°F (177°C) and prepare the streusel topping. Toss together the flour, sugar, oats, and cinnamon, then use two butter knives to cut the butter into it until the mixture resembles small peas.

Brush the tops of the loaves generously with some of the remaining egg wash and then divide the streusel topping evenly between the two loaves.

Bake for 45 minutes. Place the bread pans on a cooling rack for 5 minutes, then run a butter knife around the edges of the loaves to loosen them.

Place the pans on their sides and slide the loaves out (this should minimize the amount of streusel topping that falls off). Turn the loaves upright and cool completely before slicing.

NOTE: This bread freezes quite well when sliced. For best results, see the instructions on freezing and defrosting (page 177).

CHOCOLATE-STUFFED OAT BUNS

These are the stuff on which dreams of snow days and cozy mornings are made. My stepmom regularly doubled her oatmeal bread (page 128) so that she could make enough dough for a couple of loaves of bread, and a couple of cake pans filled with rolls of the nutty oat dough stuffed almost to bursting with pools of melted chocolate chips. When the air was brisk outside, there was absolutely nothing to compare to a mug full of creamy chai and a plate full of Chocolate-Stuffed Oat Buns.

You can, of course, halve this recipe and make a loaf of the Oatmeal Bread and one pan of the chocolatey buns, but by the same token, you can double the oatmeal bread dough and make two loaves of bread and two pans of buns. For your sake, I'll hope you're planning the latter.

Yield: 16 buns

⅓ cup (80 ml) melted butter, plus more for greasing the pans

1 batch Grandma Val's Oatmeal Sandwich Bread dough (page 128)

3 cups (500 g) bittersweet, semi-sweet, or milk chocolate chips

Grease two (8-inch [20-cm]) round cake pans with butter and set aside.

Divide the oatmeal dough into two equal-size pieces, then divide each of those into eight pieces each, rolling each piece into a ball.

Working with one ball at a time, press it into the palm of your hand, working the dough outward until you've covered your palm. Cup your palm and scoop about 2 tablespoons (31 g) of chocolate chips into the cup of your palm. Gather the edges of the dough around the chocolate chips and seal them by pressing the excess dough together.

Flip the buns, seam-side down, into the prepared pans, eight buns to a pan. Cover the pans with a clean towel and set aside to rise until they appear puffy, about 30 minutes.

While the buns are rising, preheat the oven to 350°F (177°C). Brush the tops of the buns generously with all of the melted butter and bake for 30 minutes, or until the buns are set, deeply golden brown, and smell fragrant and nutty. Let the rolls rest in the pan at room temperature for at least 5 minutes, but preferably 10 minutes, before turning out onto a cooling rack.

These are absolutely divine when eaten warm and the chocolate can ooze out over your fingers. They are also delicious when eaten cooler at room temperature, though.

CORNBREAD

Six Ways

The last type of bread we have isn't a yeast bread at all, but the one quick bread batter in our book: cornbread. It deserves to be in here standing tall alongside all of the "fancier" yeast breads because cornbread is its own category of "daily bread" (or "Daly bread" in my family because Daly was my maiden name).

I grew up on a not-at-all sweet version of cornbread that my sweet Southern grandma, Edna, preferred. Because Grandma was a saint and a cook for the ages, I also prefer her recipe for buttermilk cornbread. It's hearty, concentrated in corn flavor, and sturdy. It doesn't crumble like a lot of nonsweet cornbreads do. When it's baked in a cast-iron skillet, all it takes is one whiff of this and I'm instantly an 8-year-old girl fidgeting in my seat at Grandma's table because I can't stand to wait the 30 seconds it takes her to hand me a slice of it hot from the pan dripping with butter.

My mom made cornbread for us often like her mom did for her, and it's still one of my best-loved foods of all time. The handwritten recipe card that my grandma gave me when I was first married became one of my most treasured possessions, and I am so very happy to share her recipe with you in turn (page 136).

But cornbread isn't a one-trick pony, as great as that one trick is. You can dollop the batter over a pan full of chili for Tamale Pie (page 140). This is about as comforting as comfort food can get.

If you're looking for something with a little kick, stir in chopped pickled or candied jalapeños and cubed cheese for a Jalapeño Cheddar Cornbread (page 143)—the ultimate dish to serve alongside a pot of taco soup or chili con carne.

For cookout or picnic flair, add some chopped, grilled, or pan-fried hot dogs, and a little chopped onion into the batter for an incredible Corn Dog Bread (page 144) that you'll be proud to serve for any festive occasion.

For a variation on the theme, you can add a wee bit more sugar to Grandma Shaffer's Buttermilk Cornbread for Grandma Shaffer's Cornbread Gone Northern (page 139), a Johnny-Cake–type cornbread. That makes the ultimate in corn muffins for breakfast or snacks.

Whichever cornbread you prefer is suitable for deep-golden-brown griddle cakes; think cornbread English muffins. These Cornbread Rounds (page 147) are handy for stocking in a lunch bag with a thermos full of soup or chili, or a salad with southwestern or spicy dressing.

GRANDMA SHAFFER'S BUTTERMILK CORNBREAD

Sitting in front of a hot cast-iron skillet full of my Grandma Shaffer's Buttermilk Cornbread is my happy place. It's full of savory, concentrated corn flavor and holds together better than most nonsweet, Southern-style cornbreads. My grandma was magical and her recipes remain so. Of course, this can be cooked perfectly well in a square or round baking pan, but I love the deep brown, crispy crust that cast-iron gives this bread.

Yield: 1 (8- to 10-inch [20- to 25-cm]) cast-iron skillet or (8-inch [20-cm]) baking pan

2 tbsp (28 g) bacon grease or softened butter, for the pan

1½ cups (236 g) yellow cornmeal (not self-rising)

½ cup (63 g) all-purpose flour

1 tbsp (13 g) granulated sugar

2 tsp (9 g) baking powder

1 tsp kosher salt

¾ tsp baking soda

1¼ cups (300 ml) cultured buttermilk

2 eggs, beaten

3 tbsp (45 ml) melted butter

Preheat the oven to 425°F (220°C). Grease the bottom and sides of a cast-iron skillet or baking pan with bacon grease or softened butter. Set aside.

In a mixing bowl, whisk together the cornmeal, flour, sugar, baking powder, salt, and baking soda. In another bowl, whisk together the buttermilk, eggs, and melted butter until even. Pour the liquid mixture into the dry ingredients and use a whisk to combine until you have a smooth batter. Scrape it into the greased pan and smooth. Bake for 30 minutes, or until it is firm to the touch, golden brown, and a toothpick or butter knife inserted in the center of the bread comes out clean.

Serve warm for the best flavor. Leftovers can be stored—wrapped in a towel or plastic wrap—at room temperature for up to 48 hours, but will taste best if reheated slightly before serving.

NOTES: If you have leftover cornbread that is getting slightly stale, turn it into Cornbread Croutons (page 150).

Cornbread is another great candidate for freezing. Follow the instructions on how to freeze and defrost it (page 177) for the best results.

GRANDMA SHAFFER'S CORNBREAD GONE NORTHERN

While I definitely prefer the original, savory version of my grandma's cornbread, I know that around where I live, sweet cornbread is considered the ne plus ultra of cornbread-itude. And I love you all, so I've boosted the sugar content of Grandma's original cornbread for a lighter textured, sweet-and-corny version that I'm pretty sure my grandma would approve of anyway. Do prepare this Yankee-style cornbread in a regular baking pan instead of a cast-iron one, though. It just works better. Serve this warm drizzled with honey for the true Yankee experience.

Yield: 1 (8-inch [20-cm]) baking pan

3 tbsp (45 ml) melted butter plus 2 tbsp (28 g) softened butter for the pan

1½ cups (236 g) yellow cornmeal

¾ cup (94 g) all-purpose flour

¼ cup plus 2 tbsp (75 g) granulated sugar

2 tsp (9 g) baking powder

1 tsp kosher salt

¾ tsp baking soda

1¼ cups (300 ml) cultured buttermilk

2 eggs, beaten

Preheat the oven to 425°F (220°C). Grease the bottom and sides of a baking pan with softened butter. Set aside.

In a mixing bowl, whisk together the cornmeal, flour, sugar, baking powder, salt, and baking soda. In another bowl, whisk together the buttermilk, eggs, and melted butter until even. Pour the liquid mixture into the dry ingredients and use a whisk to combine until you have a smooth batter. Scrape it into the greased pan and smooth. Bake for 30 minutes, or until it is firm to the touch, golden brown, and a toothpick or butter knife inserted in the center of the bread comes out clean.

Serve warm for the best flavor. Leftovers can be stored—wrapped in a towel or plastic wrap—at room temperature for up to 48 hours, but will taste best if reheated slightly before serving.

NOTE: This is another great candidate for freezing. Follow the instructions on how to freeze and defrost it (page 177) for the best results.

TAMALE PIE (CORNBREAD-TOPPED CHILI)

When I was a kid, my family belonged to a church that held potlucks at least once a month. What can I say? Even in my spiritual life, I like to be fed. There was one woman (shout-out to Mrs. Robinson) who brought a tamale pie to every potluck and you could find me stationed in front of that with my plate when the prayer was over. To this day, I scout potluck tables to see if there's an equivalent of a Mrs. Robinson at a church or get-together. When I plunge that spoon down through the crust of the cornbread into the steamy hot chili, it still makes my heart skip a beat. Don't skip the unsweetened cocoa and cinnamon in this recipe. It really adds depth to the chili!

Yield: 8 servings

2 tbsp (30 ml) bacon grease or vegetable oil

2 lb (907 g) 90% lean ground beef

4 cloves garlic, minced or pressed

1 (28-oz [794-g]) can tomato puree

4 tbsp (32 g) chili powder

1 tsp ground cumin

1 tsp unsweetened cocoa

½ tsp ground cinnamon

1 (14-oz [397-g]) can pinto beans, drained and rinsed

1 (14-oz [397-g]) can black beans, drained and rinsed

1 (14-oz [397-g]) can chili beans with their liquid

2 cups (330 g) frozen corn

1 batch Grandma Shaffer's Buttermilk Cornbread batter (page 136) or Grandma Shaffer's Cornbread Gone Northern batter (page 139)

Grated cheese, for serving (optional)

Sour cream, for serving (optional)

Candied jalapeños, for serving (optional)

Preheat the oven to 400°F (200°C). Add the bacon grease or vegetable oil to a 12-inch (30-cm), oven-safe skillet over medium–high heat and then crumble in the beef. Brown the beef, breaking it up with a spoon, until it is no longer pink.

Add the garlic and stir until the garlic is fragrant, about 1 minute. Stir in the tomato puree, chili powder, cumin, cocoa, and cinnamon and bring to a boil. Simmer for 10 minutes, then stir in the pinto beans, black beans, chili beans with their liquid, and frozen corn until well combined.

Scrape the cornbread batter of your choice over the chili, smooth the batter to spread it out evenly to the edges of the skillet, and bake for 30 to 40 minutes, or until the cornbread is golden brown, a toothpick or skewer inserted into the cornbread comes out clean, and the chili is bubbling up a little around the edges.

Serve with grated cheese, sour cream, and candied jalapeños, if desired. Store leftovers tightly wrapped in the refrigerator.

JALAPEÑO CHEDDAR CORNBREAD

The name says it all, right? Oh my goodness, though, the name doesn't even cover how the spicy jalapeño pieces and smooth, melted cheddar cheese combine with the sweetness of the corn to make a cornbread that is almost a meal in and of itself. Honestly, whatever you serve with this had better be good enough to stand on its own, because this cornbread shines.

Yield: 10 to 12 servings

2 tbsp (30 ml) bacon grease or vegetable oil

½ cup (66 g) cheddar cheese, ½-inch (13-mm) dice

1 to 2 fresh jalapeños, stems and seeds removed, ⅛-inch (3-mm) dice (see Notes)

1 cup (165 g) frozen corn, thawed

1 batch Grandma Shaffer's Buttermilk Cornbread batter (page 136) or Grandma Shaffer's Cornbread Gone Northern batter (page 139)

Preheat the oven to 425°F (220°C). Grease the bottom and sides of the skillet with bacon grease or vegetable oil.

Use a spatula to stir the diced cheddar cheese, diced jalapeños, and corn into the batter. Scrape into the prepared pan and smooth the top. Bake for 30 minutes, or until it is firm to the touch, golden brown, and a toothpick or butter knife inserted in the center of the bread comes out clean.

Serve warm for the best flavor. Leftovers can be stored—wrapped in a towel or plastic wrap—at room temperature for up to 48 hours, but it will taste best if reheated slightly before serving.

NOTES: As with most cornbread, this is an excellent candidate for freezing. For the best results, use the instructions on freezing and defrosting bread (page 177).

If you're a big fan of spice, go for two jalapeños, but if you tend to be a little more sensitive to it, stick with one.

You can omit the corn from this recipe and then use it as a spicier topper for the Tamale Pie (page 140) if that dings your chimes.

CORN DOG BREAD

My guys are crazy for corn dogs. Okay, so is their mama. There's just something so summery and festive about a corn dog. And while no one could argue that food on a stick isn't portable, you could argue that corn dogs are not super easy to make and transport to a picnic. Here's where Corn Dog Bread comes into the picture. You can bake it up, wrap the pan in a towel, and pop it in the car to take to the beach or the park or wherever you want to enjoy a day outdoors with a meal. Bring a bottle of mustard and ketchup and some napkins and you're good to go!

Yield: 12 servings

2 tbsp (30 ml) bacon grease or vegetable oil

½ tsp granulated garlic

½ tsp granulated onion

1 batch Grandma Shaffer's Cornbread Gone Northern batter (page 139)

5 fully cooked hot dogs (fresh or leftover from grilling), cut into ¼-inch (6-mm) rounds

1 to 2 fresh jalapeños, stems and seeds removed, ⅛-inch (3-mm) dice (see Notes) (optional)

½ onion, diced (optional)

Preheat the oven to 425°F (220°C). Grease the bottom and sides of the skillet with bacon grease or vegetable oil. Sprinkle the granulated garlic and onion over the cornbread batter and use a whisk to incorporate it into the batter. Switch to a spatula and stir in the hot dogs plus the jalapeños and onion, if using. Scrape into the prepared pan and smooth the top. Bake for 30 minutes, or until it is firm to the touch, golden brown, and a toothpick or butter knife inserted in the center of the bread comes out clean.

Serve warm or at room temperature for the best flavor. Leftovers must be stored tightly wrapped in the refrigerator, but have a better taste and texture when reheated slightly.

NOTES: Because most corn dogs have a sweet crust, we start with our Grandma Shaffer's Cornbread Gone Northern (page 139) as the base. If you strongly prefer nonsweet cornbread, it certainly won't hurt to use Grandma Shaffer's Buttermilk Cornbread (page 136).

If you opt to add the jalapeños, I'm going to assume you like it spicy . . . but because jalapeños can vary wildly in spice levels, it is best to sample the pepper and see just how spicy it is. Decide how much to add accordingly.

As with most cornbread, this is an excellent candidate for freezing. For the best results, use the instructions on freezing and defrosting bread (page 177).

CORNBREAD ROUNDS

One day, many years ago, my oven quit on me when the baking ignitor burned out. Fancy that. Maybe it was tired. I didn't realize it was kaput until I had already whipped up a batch of cornbread batter and I certainly wasn't going to waste it, so I turned to the stovetop, greased some muffin rings, and decided to try griddle-frying my cornbread batter. It worked like a treat! The resulting cornbread rounds had super crusty outsides and perfectly cornbread-y interiors. Success! We liked it so much that sometimes I make it that way just for the fun of it.

Yield: 12 servings

Bacon grease or oil for the rings and the griddle

1 batch of Grandma Shaffer's Buttermilk Cornbread batter (page 136) or Jalapeño Cheddar Cornbread batter (page 143)

Liberally grease a large, rectangular griddle or two large cast-iron skillets and ten muffin rings (metal or silicone). Arrange the muffin rings on the griddle or pans and turn the heat to medium–high.

Use a ladle or large spoon to scoop a scant ½ cup (120 ml) of the cornbread batter into each hot muffin ring. Lower the heat to medium-low. Allow the minibreads to cook until the cornbread is dark golden brown to medium brown on the bottom, 8 to 10 minutes. If you're in doubt as to whether the time has come to flip them, examine the surface of the batter. It should still be moist looking, but you should be able to slide the ring up without any batter pouring down the sides. Slip a spatula under the ring and cornbread, slide the ring up and off the bread, and carefully flip over.

Serve warm or at room temperature for the best flavor. Leftovers must be stored tightly wrapped in the refrigerator, but they have a better taste and texture when reheated slightly.

NOTE: You can switch out the recommended batter for Grandma Shaffer's Cornbread Gone Northern (page 139), but be aware the extra sugar in the recipe browns more quickly, so you may have a much darker end result.

Upcycling

STALE BREAD
AND LEFTOVERS

You may find yourself a little carried away with all the baking, and who can blame you? When you gain confidence as a bread baker, you look for reasons to have fresh bread around all the time.

Truth be told, I can think of more reasons to have freshly baked bread than not to have freshly baked bread! But, if you're overrun by your baking efforts, I have a few recipes to help you use up your excess bread, whether it be a small or large amount.

Homemade croutons will always be superior to the bagged ones from the grocery store. You can adjust the herbs, spices, and flavorings almost infinitely. And starting with a homemade bread will give your homemade croutons a texture unmatched by commercially available ones. With the breadth of varieties of breads in this book, you already have an incredible selection of potential crouton flavors.

Don't forget the cornbread for croutons, too. Cornbread croutons, whether made from Grandma Shaffer's Buttermilk Cornbread (page 136) or Grandma Shaffer's Cornbread Gone Northern (page 139), are an unexpected and delightful addition to southwestern or Tex-Mex salads, chili, or taco soup.

Don't forget the best breadcrumbs any recipe has ever had. Homemade breadcrumbs can be a revelation. The better the breadcrumb is that you start with, the better the end recipe will be.

Ribollita (Tuscan Bread Soup) (page 165) is another one of those recipes you'll come back to time and again. While "bread soup" may sound austere, it is one of those foods that carry both major comfort food power and a flavor punch.

And you may find yourself deliberately making extra bread so you can have Buffalo Chicken Bread (page 154), English Muffin Pizzas (page 157), and Breadcrumb-Crusted Quiche (page 158). These three recipes make admirable dinners on nights when you have little time, but still want to eat well.

Skillet Apple Charlotte (page 169) is a deliciously different apple dessert that is company-worthy but doesn't require a huge time investment. We also have the always impressive and deceptively simple Bostock (almond-crusted French toast) (page 167). It's bound to become your family's new go-to brunch dish.

HERBED CROUTONS FOR SOUPS AND SALADS

Into every salad, a little crouton must fall. Or maybe a great many croutons. I'm not judging you. I'm a crouton girl, through and through. When you start with great bread, you get great croutons, and the breads in this book make seriously excellent croutons. You can make this recipe with any of the savory breads in this book. Don't forget the cornbread, folks. Cornbread croutons are divine and have a starring role in our Cornbread Panzanella Two Ways (page 161).

Yield: 3 cups (90 g)

4 cups (140 g) bread cubes (see Notes)

¼ cup (60 ml) Garlic Olive Oil (page 173) or extra virgin olive oil

2 tsp (2 g) dried herbs (see Notes)

2 tsp (12 g) kosher salt

½ tsp freshly ground black pepper

Preheat the oven to 350°F (177°C) (or 400°F [200°C] if making cornbread croutons). Toss together the bread cubes, oil, dried herbs, salt, and black pepper on a rimmed half sheet pan. Bake for 10 to 15 minutes, or until the bread cubes feel dry to the touch and are golden brown. Let them cool completely on the sheet pan. These can be stored in a tightly sealed bag or a jar with a tight-fitting lid at room temperature for up to 5 days. Stale croutons can be refreshed by placing them back on a baking sheet in a 250°F (130°C) oven for about 20 minutes or until crunchy once again.

NOTES: If you know what kinds of salads you'll be making with the croutons, you can customize your herbs to match. For Greek salads, use oregano and/or mint. For Southwestern salads, use dried cilantro and parsley plus ½ teaspoon of ground cumin. For Italian salads, use dried Italian seasonings. Get creative!

If you're making bread cubes from any bread other than cornbread, you'll get the best results if you remove the crusts before you cut the bread into cubes.

The easiest way to cut many cubes quickly is to stack up slices of bread like cards. Cut the stack into strips, then turn the cutting board 90 degrees and cut across the strips to form cubes.

DRIED BREADCRUMBS

These are exactly what they are called: dried breadcrumbs. But they're far from boring. Imagine using Asiago Herb and Garlic Bread (page 20) crumbs for your meatballs or Bacon Cheddar Scallion Bread (page 27) crumbs for your Breadcrumb-Crusted Quiche (page 158).

You can even make this recipe from the crusts you trim from bread for recipes like our Skillet Apple Charlotte (page 169). Just keep an airtight container of your crusts in the freezer until you've accumulated enough of them to make into crumbs.

There is very little art to making dried breadcrumbs, but it does need to be done in the correct order for longest-lasting results. First you dry the bread in a low oven, even if it's stale, then you pulverize it. The commercial version of dried breadcrumbs are tested scrupulously for moisture content to make them shelf stable. At home, we lack the means to do that properly, so it's best to keep them in the freezer in a container specifically designed for keeping odors and freezer burn at bay.

Yield: 1 cup (100 g)

3 large slices bread with crust

Preheat the oven to 250°F (130°C). Tear the bread into 1-inch (3-cm) chunks and arrange them in a single layer on a half sheet pan. Leave room between the pieces to allow for air circulation. Toast the bread for about 30 minutes, depending on the type of bread. Stir every 10 minutes to check for dryness. When the bread is hard and golden brown at the edges, remove the pan from the oven and let the toast cool completely to room temperature.

Add the pieces to a food processor fitted with a metal blade. Pulse until the breadcrumbs reach your desired size and texture. Transfer the crumbs to an airtight, freezer-safe container and label. Use within 3 months for best results.

NOTES: It is important to allow the toasted bread to cool completely before pulsing in the food processor as moisture is still evaporating from it as it cools.

If you don't have a food processor, you can put your cooled toast in a sturdy zipper-top bag, squeeze the air out, and pulverize it with a hefty rolling pin to create crumbs. They'll be less uniform, but still delicious.

You can create your own "Italian" breadcrumbs by adding 1 teaspoon of Italian seasoning and ⅛ teaspoon of granulated garlic to each cup (100 g) of dried breadcrumbs and tossing to distribute. It's preferable to do this just before using, rather than before you freeze the crumbs.

BUFFALO CHICKEN BREAD

As a person who spends 5 to 6 days a week in the city of Buffalo, New York, I feel pretty darned qualified to speak on the subject of Buffalo chicken. As I mentioned in the Buffalo Chicken Soft Pretzels recipe (page 95), we don't actually call it Buffalo chicken, but hey, that's quibbling. What we can all agree on is that it's delicious, and this take on the flavor combo makes great use of leftover Braided Italian Bread (page 58). Creamy, spicy, savory Buffalo chicken is spread over chewy but tender braided bread that's split. Toasted until the chicken and cheese mixture is bubbly, this renders all Buffalo chicken fans powerless. Bring this to your game-day party and watch it disappear faster than a football scandal.

Yield: 8 servings

1 loaf Braided Italian Bread (page 58)

1 batch Buffalo Chicken Spread (page 175)

2 tbsp (17 g) bleu cheese crumbles

3 green onions, thinly sliced

Preheat the oven to 375°F (190°C). Line a half sheet pan with parchment paper or a silicone baking mat.

Split a loaf of Braided Italian Bread in half horizontally. Arrange the bread, cut-side up, on the prepared sheet pan. Divide the Buffalo Chicken Spread evenly between the two halves of bread and spread it to the edges. Scatter the bleu cheese crumbles over the bread. Bake for 25 minutes, or until the Buffalo Chicken Spread is bubbly and the edges of the bread are browned.

Remove the pan from the oven and sprinkle the green onion slices over the bread. Let stand for 5 minutes before slicing. Serve warm.

ENGLISH MUFFIN PIZZAS

By this point, it should be abundantly clear that pizza is life to me. While one might argue that nine pizza-related recipes is quite enough for one book, I argue that there is no such thing as enough ways to enjoy the wonderful world of pizza. Therefore I'm adding one more to the mix: English Muffin Pizzas. I grew up eating these and was known to squeal with excitement when my mom announced these for dinner. Whether you use English Muffins (page 83) or Toastable English Muffin Bread (page 76), these little single-serving pizzas bake up and disappear at the speed of light and use up extra bread while you're at it.

Yield: 8 pizzas

4 English Muffins, split in half, or 8 (1½-inch [4-cm]-thick) slices Toastable English Muffin Bread

3 tbsp (45 ml) Garlic Olive Oil (page 173) or extra virgin olive oil

½ cup (120 ml) pizza sauce

2 cups (226 g) shredded mozzarella cheese

OPTIONAL TOPPINGS

Pepperoni slices

Diced ham

Pineapple tidbits, well drained

Diced onions

Cooked Italian sausage crumbles

Sliced olives

Or . . . whatever floats your pizza boat!

Preheat the oven to 425°F (220°C). Line a half sheet pan with parchment paper or a silicone baking mat. Arrange the English muffins (cut-side up) or the English muffin bread on the prepared pan, leaving about ½ inch (13 mm) between the pieces to allow air to circulate. Brush the oil over the cut surfaces of the bread or muffins and toast for about 6 minutes, or until the edges of the bread are starting to turn golden and the oil is bubbling on the surface.

Remove the pan from the oven and set on a heat-proof surface. Evenly divide the pizza sauce over the muffins or bread and spread with the back of a spoon to the edges. Scatter the cheese over the tops of the muffins or bread, then add any additional toppings you like over the cheese and return the pan to the oven.

Bake for 10 to 18 minutes (depending on how browned you like your cheese). Let the pizzas cool for 3 to 5 minutes on the pans before using a spatula to transfer to a platter. Use the spatula to scrape up any crispy brown bits from the pan and toss those over the tops of the pizzas on the platter. Serve hot, warm, or at room temperature.

BREADCRUMB-CRUSTED QUICHE

Quiche is most often a bit of a production, requiring a proper piecrust. In this recipe, we replace the piecrust with a generously buttered pan coated with homemade breadcrumbs. Our recipe is a riff on classic Quiche Lorraine–type combination of Swiss cheese and ham, but you can get creative and replace it with any cheese and meat you love.

Yield: 6 servings

3 tbsp (42 g) unsalted butter, divided

1 cup (160 g) diced onions

1 cup (135 g) diced, fully cooked ham

2 tbsp (5 g) Dried Breadcrumbs (page 153)

2 cups (226 g) shredded Swiss cheese

5 large eggs

1 cup (240 ml) heavy cream

1 cup (240 ml) whole milk

½ tsp kosher salt

½ tsp ground black or white pepper

Preheat the oven to 425°F (220°C). Melt 1 tablespoon (14 g) of the butter in a large, heavy-bottomed skillet over medium–high heat. Cook the onions and ham together in the butter, stirring occasionally, until the onions are translucent and golden around the edges, about 6 minutes.

While the onions and ham cook, use the remaining 2 tablespoons (28 g) of butter to generously butter the bottom and sides of a 9½-inch (24-cm) pie plate. Sprinkle the breadcrumbs evenly over the pie plate and press them into the butter. Use a spoon to scatter the ham and onions over the breadcrumbs and sprinkle the shredded cheese over that.

In a mixing bowl, whisk together the eggs, heavy cream, whole milk, salt, and pepper until even in color. Pour the mixture over the cheese, ham, and onions. Bake until the top is golden brown and the custard is set, about 30 minutes. Cool at least 8 minutes before slicing.

NOTES: If you want to try a different meat-and-cheese combination, feel free to substitute those in equal parts for the ham and cheese. Just be sure the meat is fully cooked. Likewise, you can add some precooked vegetables to the party, just be sure they're drained of juices so you don't have a soggy quiche.

For the record, a quiche should still be just the slightest bit jiggly in the center when it comes out of the oven. As it cools, it will set up. If you prefer a sturdier quiche, leave it in the oven longer.

CORNBREAD PANZANELLA TWO WAYS

My love for croutons is so ridiculously overblown that most of my salads resemble panzanelle (bread salads) anyway. When I learned that Italy had made an art of intentionally adding loads of croutons to salads, I was an instant, 100 percent enthusiastic fan. Panzanelle are really a blank canvas, so feel free to change the ingredients. The method remains the same no matter which type you make, so here we have two recipes for the price of one. Southwestern Cornbread Panzanella and Caprese Cornbread Panzanella (page 162): both delicious and wildly different. Which will you love best?

SOUTHWESTERN CORNBREAD PANZANELLA

Yield: 4 servings

4 cups (120 g) Cornbread Croutons (page 150)

1 avocado, halved, pit removed, chopped

2 large tomatoes, cut into 1-inch (3-cm) pieces, or 1 lb (454 g) cherry tomatoes, halved

1 cup (165 g) corn (cut fresh from the cob or thawed from frozen)

1 cup (195 g) cubed pepper Jack cheese

1 bell pepper (red or yellow), stem and seeds removed, diced

3 green onions, thinly sliced

1 handful fresh cilantro leaves, roughly chopped

1 jalapeño, stem and seeds removed, minced (optional)

2 limes, juiced

¼ cup (60 ml) Garlic Olive Oil (page 173) or extra virgin olive oil

1 tbsp (15 ml) agave or honey

1 tsp kosher salt

½ tsp black pepper

Gently toss the croutons, avocado, tomatoes, corn, pepper Jack cheese, bell pepper, green onions, cilantro, and jalapeño (if using) together in a large mixing bowl. Add the lime juice, oil, agave or honey, salt, and black pepper to a small jar with a tight-fitting lid. Shake until well combined, then pour over the contents of the mixing bowl and toss gently. Let the salad stand for 5 to 10 minutes before serving to give the cornbread cubes a chance to soak up some of the dressing.

CAPRESE CORNBREAD PANZANELLA

Yield: 4 servings

5 large tomatoes, cut into 1-inch (3-cm) pieces, or 2 lb (910 g) cherry tomatoes, halved

1 shallot, finely minced (optional)

2 tbsp (30 ml) Garlic Olive Oil (page 173) or extra virgin olive oil

3 tbsp (45 ml) balsamic vinegar

1½ tsp (9 g) kosher salt or flaky sea salt

4 cups (120 g) Cornbread Croutons (page 150)

5 oz (142 g) fresh mozzarella, either small pearls or cut into small bite-size pieces

½ cup (12 g) fresh basil leaves, rolled into a cigar shape and thinly sliced

In a large mixing bowl, toss together the tomatoes, shallot (if using), oil, balsamic vinegar, and salt. Cover the bowl loosely, and let stand at room temperature for 10 minutes.

Toss the mixture well, then toss in the cornbread croutons, mozzarella, and thinly sliced basil. Let the mixture stand at room temperature, loosely covered, for 15 to 20 minutes to let the cornbread soak up the juices and to let the flavors meld.

RIBOLLITA (TUSCAN BREAD SOUP)

Everyone knows Italy does food quite well in general, but Italians are wizards at using up everything and making it taste like heaven in the process. Ribollita is a brothy, traditional Tuscan soup that is made on day one and reboiled with bread to thicken it on day two. Ribollita actually means reboiled, so there you go. While the soup here is a recipe given to me by a great cook in Tuscany, the Parmesan croutons are an add-on from yours truly that I just love with it. Don't let the long ingredient list scare you off. Once you get your vegetables chopped up, it's just a matter of adding them in the order given. Mangia!

Yield: 8 hearty servings

4 oz (114 g) pancetta or bacon, diced

2 tbsp (30 ml) Garlic Olive Oil (page 173) or extra virgin olive oil

1 large onion, peeled and diced

2 large carrots, scrubbed and diced

2 ribs celery (with leaves if available), diced

3 large cloves of garlic, thinly sliced

1 tsp kosher salt or sea salt

Pinch of crushed red pepper flakes

1 medium zucchini, diced

1 (15.5-oz [439-g]) can cannellini beans, drained and rinsed

1 (14.5-oz [411-g]) can diced tomatoes in juice

2 tbsp (32 g) tomato paste

10 to 11 oz (283 to 312 g) baby kale or mature kale leaves (stems removed) chopped

4 cups (1 L) chicken stock

½ tsp dried rosemary (or 1 sprig fresh)

½ tsp dried thyme (or 1 sprig fresh)

½ tsp dried parsley (or 1 sprig fresh)

Rind of a piece of fresh Parmesan cheese (optional, but tasty)

Place the pancetta in a large pot placed over medium heat. Cook, stirring frequently, until the pancetta is golden brown and the fat has rendered out into the pan, about 5 minutes. Add the olive oil, then add the onion, carrots, celery, garlic, salt, and crushed red pepper flakes. Stir and drop the heat to medium-low. Sweat the vegetables, stirring frequently, until they begin to soften, 7 to 10 minutes. Stir in the zucchini and cook for another 3 minutes. Add the cannellini beans, diced tomatoes, and tomato paste. Stir well, then add the kale, chicken stock, rosemary, thyme, parsley, and Parmesan rind, if using. The kale may be mounding above the top rim of the stockpot. Don't worry. It will shrink to almost nothing! Raise the heat to medium-high and bring to a boil. After it boils, drop the heat to medium-low and let it simmer gently for 20 minutes.

Remove the sprigs of thyme and rosemary, then add the bread cubes and stir. Continue to simmer for 10 minutes, or until the bread has fallen apart and thickened the soup. Remove from the heat and stir in the chiffonade of basil.

(continued)

4 thick slices stale Braided Italian Bread (page 58), World's Fastest Sandwich Bread (page 15), or Super Speedy Potato Bread (page 23)

4 fresh basil leaves, rolled up into a tube and thinly sliced

PARMESAN SOUP CROUTONS

8 thick slices Braided Italian Bread (page 58), World's Fastest Sandwich Bread (page 15), Super Speedy Potato Bread (page 23), Asiago Herb and Garlic Bread (page 20), or Spinach Parmesan Bread (page 19)

2 tbsp (30 ml) Garlic Olive Oil (page 173) or extra virgin olive oil

1 cup (80 g) freshly grated Parmesan cheese

TO PREPARE THE PARMESAN SOUP CROUTONS

Turn the broiler of your oven on high. Brush both sides of the pieces of bread with the olive oil. Place the bread on a rack 6 inches (15 cm) under the broiler and toast until golden brown. Flip the bread over, mound the top of each slice of bread with 2 tablespoons (10 g) of freshly grated Parmesan cheese, and return the pan under the broiler until the cheese is bubbly, melted, and golden brown in places.

TO SERVE THE RIBOLLITA

Ladle the Ribollita into serving bowls and top each serving with a Parmesan Soup Crouton.

NOTE: You can make the soup one day ahead up to the point where you remove the sprigs of fresh herbs (if you used them). After you reboil it, stir in the bread cubes and simmer until the bread has fallen apart, then stir in the thinly sliced basil.

BOSTOCK

This twist on a classic French pastry, brioche aux amandes, can be made by the most beginner of all beginners; no pastry chef training is necessary. It usually has loosened apricot jam on day-old brioche, which is then topped with almond paste made from almond meal, butter, sugar, almond extract, and eggs (frangipane), plus a fistful of sliced almonds, and is baked until the top and bottom are golden brown and crisped and the inside is soft. It's dusted generously with powdered sugar and is, simply put, divine.

Yield: 10 servings

10 (1-inch [3-cm]-thick) slices day-old or two-day-old Pillowy Soft Sandwich Bread (page 112) or brioche

3 tbsp (60 g) apricot jam or preserves

1 tbsp (15 ml) Grand Marnier liqueur

1½ cups (125 g) almond meal

¾ cup (170 g) unsalted butter, softened to room temperature

¾ cup (150 g) granulated sugar

1 egg

½ tsp almond extract

Pinch of salt

1 cup (92 g) sliced almonds

Powdered sugar, for dusting

Preheat the oven to 400°F (200°C).

Arrange the bread slices on half sheet pans, leaving just a little room between the pieces.

Heat the apricot jam or preserves in a saucepan over very low heat or in a microwave-safe bowl in 10-second bursts, stirring after each one, until loose and hot. Add the Grand Marnier and stir well until evenly combined.

Divide the preserve mixture evenly between the slices of bread. Spread the preserve mixture evenly over the bread to the edges and let it soak into the bread while you prepare the frangipane.

Using a sturdy spoon, hand mixer, or stand mixer, mix the almond meal, butter, sugar, egg, almond extract, and salt until it forms a cohesive, smooth paste. Divide the mixture evenly between the slices of bread, using a butter knife to spread it evenly to the edges.

Sprinkle the almonds over the frangipane, then bake until the tops are set and puffy and golden brown, 16 to 24 minutes. Dust generously with powdered sugar and serve warm or at room temperature.

Leftovers can be stored wrapped or in a loosely covered container at room temperature for 3 days. To refresh the Bostock and serve warm, preheat the oven to 350°F (177°C) and heat the Bostock on a sheet pan just until warmed through.

(See photo on page 186.)

SKILLET APPLE CHARLOTTE

Apple Charlotte is a dessert traditionally made by dipping stale bread in melted butter, lining a bowl or mold, and filling it with stewed apples before weighing it down and baking it. My version is much faster and easier, but still uses up stale bread in the most delightful, caramelly way. An ovenproof skillet, a handful of apples, a few slices of stale bread, some butter, maple syrup or honey, and a smidgen of sugar are all that's needed to create a dish of sweet, caramelized apples with a crisp, buttery crust that's turned out onto a dish like a tarte tatin. When topped with a dollop of whipped cream or scoop of ice cream, this dessert is easy and comforting enough for any day, but it's sophisticated enough for special occasions.

Yield: 6 servings

5 to 6 (¼-inch [6-mm]) slices stale white bread, crusts removed

4 medium-size apples, peeled, cored, and cut into 8 wedges each

5 tbsp (70 g) unsalted butter, divided

¼ cup (60 ml) maple syrup, preferably dark Grade B

2 tsp (8 g) granulated sugar or raw sugar

¼ cup (80 g) peach or apricot preserves, orange marmalade, or apple jelly

Preheat the oven to 400°F (200°C).

Arrange the bread in a square on a cutting board and lay an oven-safe, 10-inch (25-cm) skillet face down over the top of the bread. Use a small, sharp knife to cut the bread into the shape of the skillet by cutting around the perimeter of the skillet. Place the skillet on a cold burner on the stove. Nestle the apple slices snugly against each other in the pan with the cored edges facing up.

Cut 3 tablespoons (42 g) of butter into small cubes. Dot the butter over the apple wedges. Pour the maple syrup over the apples and turn the heat to high. Bring to a boil, put a tight-fitting lid in place, and drop the heat to low. Shimmy the pan from time to time and cook until the apples are tender, about 5 minutes.

Remove the lid from the pan, and raise the heat to high. Cook, shaking the pan every so often, until the liquid is mostly evaporated and the apples are caramelized, 7 to 8 minutes.

Arrange the bread over the apples in the pan. Melt the remaining 2 tablespoons (28 g) of butter and brush it over the bread. Sprinkle the sugar evenly over the buttered bread. Bake for 20 minutes or until the bread is deeply golden brown. Lay a heat-proof plate that extends beyond the edge of the skillet and invert it carefully so the Skillet Apple Charlotte is now on the plate. Microwave the preserves for about 30 seconds and stir to loosen. Spoon the preserves over the Skillet Apple Charlotte. Serve hot or warm.

Extra! Extra!

OTHER GOODIES TO MAKE YOUR BREAD EVEN BETTER

While bread is wonderful all by itself, there are some little extras you can throw in whether in the dough, on the dough before baking, or as a dip for your bread. In this mini chapter, I give you some fast and furious add-ins, add-ons, and dunkables.

Check out the Pumpernickel Bread Base (page 172), which is a quick way to transform an ordinary one-hour bread into Pumpernickel Sandwich Bread (page 28) and regular old bagels into Pumpernickel Bagels and Bagel Sticks (page 103). It is the only thing in this book that requires some ingredients that are slightly harder to find in local stores, but I promise both that they're easy to find at major online retailers such as Amazon and King Arthur Flour and that getting them is well worth it!

Sometimes you want a little more garlic than a recipe instructs you to use. Okay, if you're me, you almost always want a little more garlic. That's where our Garlic Olive Oil (page 173) comes into play. It's easy as can be to whip up and makes everything it touches taste better.

Sun-Dried Tomato Pesto (page 174) is a dip that's also a spread and an ingredient. This stuff is like a little black dress for bread. Whether you put it in or on your bread, you're going to go nuts for it. Don't settle for just putting it in, on, or with your bread; you can also dollop it into vegetable soups, or use it as a spread for sandwiches, burgers, and wraps. It can also be used in place of pizza sauce.

Everything Bagel Topping (page 172) is all the rage now and can be purchased at many grocers, but when you make it yourself, you can tinker with the ingredients and add as much or as little of every component as you'd like! It is also less expensive per pound (454 g) when you make it yourself, so you can toss it on, well, everything!

Chai Spice Blend (page 173) is a lovely combination of spices that warm you from the inside out and taste like a hot cup of chai; cinnamon, cardamom, allspice, nutmeg, cloves, and one little surprise spice that you might not expect but is delicious. I use this as a shortcut to adding big autumnal flavor to baked goods like our Chai Spiced Monkey Bread (page 123), Harvest Spice Apple Bread (page 31), and Cinnamon Swirl Streusel-Topped Oat Bread (page 131).

Don't forget the Buffalo Chicken Spread (page 175)! You can serve this cold as a dip, as a sandwich spread, or slathered over Buttery Soft Pretzels (page 86) or split Braided Italian Bread (page 58) and bake until hot and bubbly for the ultimate in game-day snacking.

PUMPERNICKEL BREAD BASE

You are going to love the bread you make with this bread base. It's full of the ingredients that transform basic breads into a tangy, chewy pumpernickel reminiscent of those you find at NYC bakeries and delis.

Yield: about 3 cups (365 g)

Whisk the pumpernickel flour, caramel color powder, sourdough flavor, and powdered deli rye flavor until even in color. Store in an airtight container in a cool, dry place for up to a year.

2½ cups (9.375 oz [266 g], by weight) pumpernickel flour

⅓ cup (1.5 oz [43 g], by weight) caramel color powder

4 heaping tbsp (1.5 oz [43 g], by weight) sourdough flavor

2 tbsp (0.5 oz [14 g], by weight) powdered deli rye flavor

EVERYTHING BAGEL TOPPING

I'm giving you my favorite ratio of seeds and seasonings combined, but feel free to tinker with this mix until you make it exactly what you love. Heads-up: leaving out the salt will improve the holding power of any baked good you top with this blend.

Yield: about ¾ cup (120 g)

Add all of the ingredients to an 8-ounce (227-g) jar with a tight-fitting lid or in a zipper-top bag. Shake well until everything is evenly combined. Store in a cool, dry place for up to a year.

3 tbsp (24 g) sesame seeds

3 tbsp (31 g) poppy seeds

3 tbsp (30 g) dried minced garlic

3 tbsp (15 g) dried minced onions

1 tbsp (18 g) coarse pretzel salt (optional)

GARLIC OLIVE OIL

This is the stuff, friends. I go through about a quart (0.9 L) of this per month. I use it in bread, on bread, as a dipping sauce for bread, on pasta, in salad dressings, and so much more. You can use it straight from the refrigerator, or allow it to loosen up at room temperature before using it.

Yield: 1 cup (240 ml)

1 cup (240 ml) olive oil

8 cloves garlic, peeled but left whole

Place the oil and the garlic cloves in a small, heavy-bottomed saucepan and place the pan over very low heat. Watch the oil closely to make sure the garlic is not burning. Simmer for about 30 minutes. Move the pan off the heat and use a spatula to gently press on the garlic cloves. Cover the pan and let it infuse for 30 minutes. Strain the oil through a fine mesh sieve into a jar that has a tight-fitting lid. Store in the refrigerator for up to a month.

CHAI SPICE BLEND

This spice blend is like a warm blanket on a cool fall day. It's 100 percent delicious and can be used in just about anything that calls for ground cinnamon.

Yield: about ½ cup (62 g)

4 tbsp (31 g) ground cinnamon

2 tbsp (10 g) ground ginger

2 tsp (4 g) ground allspice

½ tsp ground nutmeg

¼ tsp ground cloves

¼ tsp ground black pepper

Whisk the cinnamon, ginger, allspice, nutmeg, cloves, and black pepper in a small bowl. Scoop into a small jar with a tight-fitting lid. Store in a cool, dark place for up to 1 year.

SUN-DRIED TOMATO PESTO

It's the flavor of summer and Italy all rolled into one with the concentrated tomato goodness of sun-dried tomatoes, loads of fresh basil, pesto, and Parmesan cheese blitzed to form a spread you'll keep on hand all the time. Use as a dip for vegetables, pretzels, pita chips, tortilla chips; as a spread for sandwiches, burgers, and wraps; in place of pizza sauce; or dolloped in Italian-style soups for added flavor boosts. It's the herby, garlicky flavor punch of the very best kind that goes into our Sun-Dried Tomato Pesto Pinwheel Rolls (page 70), too!

Yield: about 3 cups (720 ml)

1 (8.5-oz [241-g]) jar julienne-cut sun-dried tomatoes with herbs packed in oil

1 (14.5-oz [411-g]) jar fire-roasted diced tomatoes

1 cup (252 g) prepared basil pesto

1 cup (80 g) grated Parmesan cheese

12 fresh basil leaves torn into pieces

Add the jar of sun-dried tomatoes and their oil and the diced tomatoes and their juices to a food processor fitted with a metal blade. Process until the contents are a uniform paste but not smooth. Add the pesto, Parmesan cheese, and torn basil leaves to the paste and pulse until the pesto and cheese are evenly incorporated. Scrape into a jar with a tight-fitting lid and store in the refrigerator for up to 10 days.

BUFFALO CHICKEN SPREAD

This spicy Buffalo chicken spread is great cold or spread onto soft pretzels or split bread and baked until bubbly. If you really dislike bleu cheese you can omit it, but don't tell the people of Buffalo; we're liable to throw elbows when it comes to bleu cheese.

Yield: 6 cups (1.4 L)

4 oz (113 g) cream cheese, softened to room temperature

8 oz (227 g) shredded cheddar cheese

4 cups (560 g) chopped, cooked chicken

6 green onions, thinly sliced

1 cup (224 g) mayonnaise

¾ cup (180 ml) Buffalo sauce

½ cup (123 g) bleu cheese crumbles

Using a hand mixer, stand mixer, or sturdy spoon, mix together the cream cheese, cheddar cheese, chicken, green onions, mayonnaise, Buffalo sauce, and bleu cheese crumbles until they form a cohesive paste. Store in an airtight container in the refrigerator for up to a week.

Bread Geek:
UNLOCKING THE SECRETS OF GREAT BREAD

HOW TO SHAPE ROUND LOAVES OR ROLLS

This is not tricky, but there is a trick to it. Whether you're making a large, round loaf or small dinner rolls, the process is basically the same. Lift the dough. Gently pull the edges of the dough down and tuck it under. Turn the dough one-quarter turn and repeat. Do this until you've formed a cohesive round. Place the round on the clean surface and cup your hands at an angle around the edges. Allow your hands to gently tighten the dough down over the surface as you turn the dough in a circle in one direction. When you're done, the dough should look taught and round. Place on the prepared pans.

HOW TO FREEZE AND DEFROST BREAD

Most of the breads in this book are suitable for freezing for eating at a later date. It's not difficult to be able to pull bread from the freezer and have it taste like freshly baked bread. However, because it is prone to picking up rogue odors in the freezer, and can dry out quickly if defrosted incorrectly, there are a few steps you can take to ensure the best results.

First, make sure your bread is fully cooled to room temperature before wrapping it up. This allows the crumb to finish setting up and will help avoid sogginess in your defrosted bread. You can either freeze it whole or slice it to make grabbing a slice or two without wrangling the whole loaf easier.

Wrap your bread in a double layer of plastic wrap, then a single layer of aluminum foil to avoid freezer burn. While you're at it, you can help stave off the bread absorbing any odors by sliding that triple-wrapped loaf of happiness into a zipper-top freezer bag. If you've sliced the bread for easier access, you'll want to just stick with the double plastic wrap and a zipper-top bag.

There are three different methods to defrost or thaw your bread, depending on what you want to do with it.

THE COLD DEFROST METHOD

All you need to do is place the wrapped loaf of bread on the counter and leave it there until it comes to room temperature. The bread will re-absorb any moisture in the wrapper and be deliciously fresh. This is the best method to use when you want to eat a loaf during a couple of days. It's the gentlest way to defrost a loaf of bread.

If you want to revitalize and refresh it, you can wrap the completely room temperature loaf in foil and pop it into a preheated 350°F (177°C) oven for 5 to 10 minutes.

In my opinion, this is the best and the easiest of the three methods. It is my recommended method for whole loaves of bread.

THE HOT THAW METHOD

Remove the foil carefully, reserving it. Take off and discard both layers of plastic wrap. Rewrap the loaf in the foil. Place directly on the rack in a preheated 350°F (177°C) oven. Warm for about 20 minutes, or until the bread is warm to the touch.

This is a great method to defrost and refresh a loaf when you know you're in a hurry and know you're going to eat it quickly. Keep in mind that a loaf thawed this way does go stale more rapidly than with the cold defrost method.

THE TOASTER METHOD

Remove as many slices as you desire and put them directly into the toaster. It will thaw and toast simultaneously.

This is the optimal method for single slices of bread if you opted to slice the loaf before freezing it.

A BRIEF DISCUSSION OF INGREDIENTS USED IN THIS BOOK

Find a brand of flour that gives you consistent results, and stick with it. For me, I use King Arthur Flour exclusively for my all-purpose flour, bread flour, and whole wheat flour, but am a little more experimental when it comes to my semolina flour. Try out different brands as you experiment and learn what you love best.

ALL-PURPOSE FLOUR

I'm willing to bet you probably already have at least a partial 5-pound (2.27-kg) bag of this in your pantry. It is made from milled hard winter wheat. It is the most commonly purchased flour in the United States for a good reason; it is good for almost any recipe that uses flour. In most recipes, you can substitute this for bread flour if it is all you have. The end product will be slightly different in rise and texture, but it will still be delicious.

BREAD FLOUR

Bread flour has a higher percentage of protein in it than all-purpose flour and is made from hard spring wheat. The higher protein allows more gluten to develop and absorbs more liquid in the recipe. This results in baked goods with slightly more "chew" and structure, tighter crumb, and a higher rise. For optimal results, please use this when the recipe calls for it.

In a pinch, you can substitute all-purpose flour for bread flour, but the reverse is not necessarily always true. Sometimes the protein content in bread flour is too high (the flour is "too strong") to substitute for all-purpose flour; for instance, in cornbread, cakes, and cookies.

A good rule of thumb is to look at how much kneading takes place. If it is a bread recipe that requires a lot of kneading (3 minutes or more by hand or machine), then bread flour should work. If it is a no-knead bread, where you do not have time to develop the gluten by kneading, most often you should stick to all-purpose flour. Of course, there are exceptions to this (most yeast bread recipes are good candidates for subbing in all-purpose flour), but it's a good guideline to keep in mind.

WHOLE WHEAT FLOUR

This is what it sounds like; the whole wheat berry is ground to make this flour. It is a nuttier, coarser flour that has more nutrients intact than all-purpose or bread flour. The two most common types of whole wheat flour sold are ground from hard red spring wheat (whole wheat flour) or hard white spring or winter wheat (white whole wheat flour).

Contrary to what you might think, white whole wheat flour is not white flour, it is simply made from white wheat. It is still a whole grain flour. Because of the type of wheat it is milled from, it is milder in flavor and paler in color than its whole wheat flour cousin. These two flours can be used interchangeably, according to personal preference.

That said, any whole wheat flour behaves a little differently than all-purpose or bread flour in bread recipes, so you can't wholesale substitute all whole wheat flour willly-nilly. It is far lower in gluten than all-purpose or bread flour, so dough made from it does not rise as high or as fast.

To aid in texture, recipes that use whole wheat flour often call for a mixture of whole wheat flour and all-purpose—or better yet, in my opinion—bread flour. The higher protein in those flours help create structure and rise that the whole wheat bread would otherwise lack, plus it moves the process along much faster.

TYPE "00" FLOUR

This is a very chilled-out flour. Think all-purpose flour minus the type A personality. It's a lower protein, lower gluten flour that is used in Italy for pizzas and pastas. It yields a silky dough that is very easy to work with and doesn't fight back as much when you try to roll it or stretch it. If you can't find it or the budget doesn't allow it, you can substitute all-purpose flour in most recipes without a huge difference. If you are looking for the most authentically Italian-style pizza crust or best wood-fired pizza crust, you'll want to stick with the "00" flour, though!

SEMOLINA "FLOUR"

This golden hued, coarsely ground grain is not technically a flour at all, but is often sold as "semolina flour." It looks very much like cornmeal but is made from grinding the endosperm of durum wheat. While it may sound unfamiliar, I promise you've had it before if you've ever eaten dried pasta or couscous. It is very high in gluten, making it a natural addition to chewy, Italian-style breads like our Braided Italian Bread (page 58).

In almost all cases, it is not interchangeable with other flours and should be used as directed. While there may be other products marketed as semolina—such as Cream of Wheat, "rice" semolina, and "corn" semolina—these are not able to be substituted in a recipe calling for semolina unless specifically noted.

Because of its fine, sandy texture, it is also excellent for using under pizza dough on a peel to act like ball bearings and to keep it sliding easily. I also sometimes use it in place of cornmeal to coat the insides of the pans when making English Muffin Bread (page 76) or English Muffins (page 83).

PUMPERNICKEL BREAD BASE

The Pumpernickel Bread Base (page 172) is used in two recipes that I consider "must make" recipes in the book: Pumpernickel Sandwich Bread (page 28) and Pumpernickel Bagels (page 103). You can also make Mini Bread Bowls for Soups and Stews (page 35) and Herbed Croutons for Soups and Salads (page 150) with the Pumpernickel Sandwich Bread (page 28) dough and leftover bread, respectively.

Each of the following items might not be available at your local grocer, but they are all available through online retailers like King Arthur Flour, Amazon.com, Authentic Foods, and may be available at bulk food stores near you, too.

Pumpernickel flour, also known as whole rye flour, is a mineral-rich, high-fiber flour ground from the germ and bran of rye berries or grains from rye grass. It has a distinct flavor that those who love it crave.

Powdered caramel coloring is one of the oldest and longest used food colorings. It's made when carbohydrates (molasses, invert sugars, glucose, etc.) are heat treated. In other words, they're very carefully brought to the point of burning. This creates the deep, dark, chocolatey brown and slight bitterness that we associate with pumpernickel bread. This is the only ingredient in the Pumpernickel Bread Base (page 172) that can be omitted from the mixture without seriously affecting the final texture, but you will lose the luscious color and some of the little background of bitterness that is desirable in pumpernickel bread.

Powdered sourdough flavor is a shortcut to great sourdough flavor and texture without having to use or maintain a sourdough starter. A couple of tablespoons gives bread that zesty tang and some of the chewy texture characteristic of a good West Coast sourdough. This is a crucial ingredient in the Pumpernickel Bread Base (page 172) and is easily found online through retailers like King Arthur Flour and Amazon.com.

Powdered deli rye flavoring is the final "secret" ingredient in our Pumpernickel Bread Base. It gives your pumpernickel breads that certain je ne sais quoi that makes sourcing these ingredients well worth it. It's tangy, but has a different kind of tang than the sourdough flavor. It makes your bread taste like it came from a NYC deli. And for what it's worth, don't inhale deeply to smell this stuff when you open the bag. It's pretty strong smelling, but really subtle when you add it to the bread.

. . . and finally . . .

YEAST

This is really what it's all about, right? This is the ingredient that freaks people out, if they're going to be worried about bread baking, but it's just an ingredient! I buy yeast in bulk, 1-pound (454-g) packages from online retailers or bulk food stores, but it is just fine to purchase it in premeasured packets at the grocery store.

In yeast, as with flour, bread bakers tend to be a brand-loyal lot. For my almost daily bread baking, I rely on the consistent results I get from 1-pound (454-g) packages of SAF-Instant or Red Star Active Dry Yeast. This is another ingredient with which I encourage you to experiment to find your favorite.

The recipes in this book call for specific amounts of yeast that often differ from the quantities in the individual packets, so **be sure to measure your yeast according to recipe instructions**.

I store yeast in the refrigerator in an airtight canning jar. Because yeast is a living thing that has been freeze-dried into dormancy, it needs consistent, cool storage temperatures for the most consistent results in your baking.

Yeast is the ingredient that does the power-lifting in bread, so treat it right and it will give you the results you need. Because it is a living thing, it can be a little capricious. Some days it will take longer to rise than at other times. This is less of an issue in quick-rise bread doughs like all of our one-hour breads, because there is enough yeast in there to lift a sleepy teen out of bed, but in recipes that are not designed to be done in one hour and in recipes with higher amounts of whole wheat, you may need to exercise patience and your powers of observation rather than your timer skills.

EQUIPMENT

You can really get away with a mixing bowl, half sheet pans, and a sturdy spoon, but I do reference more equipment than that in the book. Below you'll find a list of the equipment called for in the book along with a few words about why they're handy. I use every item on this list regularly.

Mixing bowl. It's best to make this bigger than you think you'll need for a multitude of reasons. If you're keeping a minimalist kitchen, you want a bowl that can handle any task you throw at it. Make this mixing bowl a giant, heavy-gauge stainless steel one and you'll have a bowl big enough to rise any batch of dough, house a meal-size salad, bake a cake in (in a pinch) and use as a Chihuahua bath. Don't worry. I didn't bathe my Chihuahua in my mixing bowl, but if I needed to, I could.

Half sheet pans. I would write a love song to half sheet pans if I was a songwriter. These are the workhorses of my kitchen and I often reach for them multiple times a day. These, lined with parchment, are my preferred pans for cooking all but one of the one-hour bread recipes. I also use them for pizzas, rolls, braided bread, sheet-pan meals, cooking bacon, and much, much more. If you're strictly minimalist, though, they still rock without parchment.

Kitchen scale. While this is not technically necessary, I do highly recommend owning a kitchen scale that has the ability to tare. What this means is that you can place your bowl on the scale then hit "zero" or "tare" and it ignores the bowl so you can measure your flour without doing math to subtract the weight of the bowl from the reading you get off the scale. You can get one of these for less than $10 from big box stores or online retailers.

Silicone baking mats a.k.a. Silpats. I prefer using these to line the pans when I make soft pretzels because pretzels have a tendency to stick to parchment and nude pans. These are a marginally higher ticket item available in a range of prices and sizes, but they're indispensable in my kitchen. There are many non–name brand ones available now at a much lower price than they used to be; you may be able to find a 2-pack for $8 on a major online retailer, for example.

Bench knife and dough scraper. A bench knife is more rigid for better cutting and scraping of flat surfaces while a dough scraper has enough flexibility to get into rounded areas and crevices of bowls. Both are fantastic for cutting dough into pieces and are economical and indispensable.

Dough whisk. This is absolutely not necessary in any world, but it is definitely on my list of things I love. It makes quick work of blending slack, no-knead doughs like our Best Pan Pizza Dough (page 39) and English Muffin Bread (page 76). It's also wonderful for pancake batter, cake batter, and anything else that you don't want to overmix.

Fish spatula. You may be wondering what a fish spatula is doing on a baking accoutrements list, but I promise you're going to love this. Not only is it great for (surprise) FISH, but the slatted, semi-flexible spatula is also excellent for lifting bagels and soft pretzels out of their boiling water bath, and it's great for easing into a pan and under the edge of the first ham and cheese or cinnamon roll. They're sturdy enough not to collapse under the weight of something delicious, but they're also flexible enough to avoid mangling delicate, fresh-from-the-oven baked goods as you transfer them to a cooling rack.

Rolling pin. I'm going to let you in on a secret. Those rolling pins that spin on an axis with little handles on the end are not what you want in your kitchen. I know they're cute and quaint, but this is another science moment. You waste all that energy spinning the roller on the pin, when you could transfer the energy directly to rolling out the dough. I highly recommend a French-style rolling pin, which is basically a glorified 1½-inch (38-mm) dowel. These are also available in a range of prices from $10 on up to eye-popping prices. No need to get fancy, though. That $10 one will do the job just fine. And if you'd like, you can make your own by sanding a nice fat dowel yourself. Just be sure to brush off the dust and oil it well before you start using it.

Pastry mat. This is a silicone mat that has measurements on it. I use it as a surface for kneading, rolling out, cutting, and/or shaping dough. The measurements let me know the length and width of the dough I've rolled out, or how large a circle I've made. It also gives me a visual when I'm trying to cut dough into equal-size pieces. This one is not expensive luxury at about $12, but it is a luxury nonetheless. Can I do without it? Absolutely. But I don't want to do without it.

Instant read thermometer. These eliminate all of the guesswork sometimes involved in discerning whether a loaf of bread is done in the center. Unless otherwise specified, every bread in this book is done when the center measures at least 190°F (88°C). These can be purchased for as little as $4 for a basic model or as much as you're willing to spend for one that has technological bells and whistles.

Pizza stone. Allow these handy-dandy flat stones to heat up with your oven for the perfect pizza-cooking surface for homemade, artisan-style, hand-stretched pizzas. But you don't have to sweat finding a place to store them. They can take up permanent residence in your oven and serve as a great way to regulate heat and eliminate hot spots. You can put pans on them and bake on them just like you would on your oven rack.

Pizza peel. If you're cooking on a pizza stone or in a wood-fired pizza oven, you're going to want one or more of these. They're basically glorified, heat-proof, giant spatulas.

Oven gloves. Stick with me on this one. I have burned my hands countless times through thin spots in oven mitts or had hot pads slip leaving me grabbing a scorching hot pan. I happily discovered knitted oven gloves with silicone nonslip grip on them. They aren't necessarily cute, but what they lack in flair, they more than make up for in protection. These bad boys protect your entire hand and wrist to well over temperatures home ovens can hit and cannot slip off. I wouldn't be without these for love nor money.

Bread pans. It's true that many of the breads in this book can be cooked on a regular old rimmed sheet pan, but sometimes you just want a classic loaf shape. For the sake of ease, **all loaf pans referred to in this book are a standard 8½ x 4½ x 3–inch (22 x 11 x 8–cm) size**. When purchased brand new, loaf pans can be as inexpensive as $4. More "cutting-edge" or specialized-shape pans can be more expensive. If you get them at yard sales, you can get them far less expensively than that. My preference is for aluminized steel pans. The ones I love are coated with silicone coating that almost guarantees an easy release of bread baked in them. Their thick walls ensure that the heat is distributed evenly, helping mitigate any issues with hot spots in ovens.

Cast-iron skillet. Yes, they're heavy. No, they don't nest nicely with other pans. Yes, they require a little special care, but boy, there is no cornbread like the cornbread cooked in a cast-iron skillet. I also use that same skillet for Best Pan Pizza (page 39), Sun-Dried Tomato Pesto Pinwheel Rolls (page 70), and Skillet Apple Charlotte (page 169). Thankfully, these are another pretty budget-friendly kitchen addition. Brand new, a 12-inch (30-cm) cast-iron skillet can run anywhere from $13 up.

Baking pans. I have an aluminized metal 9 x 13–inch (23 x 33–cm) rectangular pan that I use for Detroit-Style Pizza (page 48). Can you cook that in a regular old metal 9 x 13? Yes. But you get that extra-crisp crust with the blackened cheese edges in the aluminized metal pan that the standard metal pan just can't quite match. I love my aluminized steel one for the same reason I love that construction in a loaf pan. I also have and regularly use an 8 x 8–inch (20 x 20–cm) pan and a set of three 8-inch (20-cm) round cake pans made the same way. Between those, the cast-iron pans, and the half sheet pans, these are all my kitchen really needs.

Stand mixer. Yep, this is one of the big-ticket items. I highly recommend using a stand mixer that comes with a batter blade, dough hook, and whisk attachments. This is an investment, to be sure, but one worth considering if you do a lot of baking. It makes fast work of kneading dough, freeing up your hands for other tasks. Some recipes (for example, bagels) are significantly easier to make in a stand mixer than by hand. It isn't strictly necessary, but it sure is helpful!

Wood-fired pizza oven. This is another luxury, to be certain, but it might be more affordable than you think. There are small, portable, wood-pellet–fueled pizza ovens available through major online retailers that run less than $300. Like I said, it's pricey, but if you're a wood-fired pizza maniac, this is a bit of indulgence you might want to consider. The bare-bones model we have heats up to more than 900°F (480°C) in less than 10 minutes and cooks a full-size 12-inch (30-cm) pizza in about 1 minute flat.

ACKNOWLEDGMENTS

To my Foodie with Family readers: I owe all of you a massive debt of gratitude. There is nothing I love more than knowing you're feeding those you love with food I serve to those I love. It makes my day when I hear from you. Thank you!

To my husband: First and foremost, I need to say a gigantic thank you to you for being willing to do the cookbook waltz with me once again. You were the most intrepid taste-tester. Together, we expanded our comfort zone with comfort waistbands while I wrote this book. And I understand why you asked in all seriousness whether I'd consider titling my next cookbook *Carrots and Kale: Together at Last*. To you I say, "No way. But I love you bigger than my stretchy pants," and that's saying something. Plus, you're cute. I love you, my forever sweetheart. Also, let's go for a run together. I mean, after a loooooooong nap, of course.

To my boys, Liam, Aidan, Ty, Leif, and Rowan: Thanks for doing the monstrous amounts of extra pots and pans that I dirtied while writing this book. And thank you guys for being the best human garbage disposals a mom could ever want. You guys are princes among men and have been since you were born. I'm proud to be your mother. Also, if I catch any of you breathing fire (looking at two of you), hurtling down the road on a chair balanced on a piece of plywood balanced on a skateboard, getting your tonsils removed in another country, throwing a card at your brother's eyeball, riding off on a bike without telling anyone where you're going, or feeding the trolls at a professional sporting event (AGAIN to all of those), you're going to be in very big trouble. I love you.

To my daughter-in-law, Anaïs: Thank you for being my first girl. I look forward to a lifetime of snacks and book recommendations with you and seeing you and Liam build a family together. I'm so glad you're here. *Tu est vraiment ma belle-fille et une belle fille.*

To my mom, Cathy, and my dad, Jim: Thank you for being my biggest cheering section through my entire life and for teaching me the inestimable value of being seriously silly rule-questioners. I love you both bigger than the bay forever.

To my sisters, Jessamine, Christina, and Airlia, and my brothers, Luke and Nathaniel: Thanks for being my original friends and most worthy board-game adversaries. You guys are the best people ever to break toes with, break bread with, break camp with, and break, um, other stuff with. Also, there is no one better qualified to quote the entirety of *The Three Amigos* or *Breakin'* than you guys. I love, admire, and respect all of you.

To my aunts and uncles: You are the best. You have always made me feel loved and worthy. I'm awfully lucky to have you in my corner.

To my Lindamood clan: Thank you for being you. I can always count on you for belly-laughs and sweet memories.

To Alison Santora: Thank you for trekking all the way here from Mexico to watch Sister Wendy, drink wine, eat snacks, and be for me who you have been since we met way back when: a friend with whom there is always comfort, love, and the best book recommendations. I love you so much! Here's to 3x the 30 years we already have as kindred spirits. Um, 30 years? Hold me.

To Mary Younkin and Meseidy Rivera: We are the three amigas. We've passed the statistical friendship hurtle, so you guys are stuck with me for life. Thank you for being my sounding boards. Also, thank you for being my single greatest source of belly-laugh–inducing GIFs. All joking aside, I love you guys. I'm grateful. Without you I'd be lost. You're the bestest of all the peoples.

To my cousin Jenny-Meade: We don't get to see each other nearly enough, but I'm grateful that no matter how much time passes between our visits, it still feels like it did when we were little girls strolling down dirt roads by the lake and telling each other our hopes and dreams. I love you.

To my editor Marissa Giambelluca and the entire crew at Page Street Publishing: Thank you for taking not just one, but two chances on me and making it possible for me to have two books of which I am terrifically proud to my name. My husband has asked that my next book be called *Carrots and Kale: Together at Last*. He's breaded out.

To my friends at Neglia Ballet Artists (Kimberly, Bronwen, Leela, Michelle, Heidi, and Sergio): Thank you for letting me park myself at the table in the breakroom to type uninterrupted. Thank you for being my field taste-testers, for testing recipes for me, and for making life fun and interesting. P.S. Thanks for taking all that bread off my hands. I'm grateful for you all.

To my Grandma Shaffer, my stepmom, Valerie, and my mother-in-law, Dolores: I'm so thankful for all the love you showed me and grateful for the time I had with all of you, but wish it had been longer. Grandma, you were the ultimate baker and your bread set me on a lifelong love affair with homemade bread. Thank you for always setting aside a basket of rolls for me. Val, you showed me how to make homemade bread a part of my daily (and Daly) life and the joy of viewing a loaf of homemade bread as an essential tool in "How to Cook a Wolf." Dolores, you always made me feel welcomed, loved, and valued. I love and miss you all.

To my blogger friends who are real-life friends and too numerous to name: You guys inspire me every single day to work better, be a better person, make better food, and take better photos. Thank you for sharing your knowledge and being my tribe.

To my friend Carolyn Panzica: Thank you for raising an amazing young man, for being an intrepid taste-tester, for being terribly naughty, and for being my friend.

To Lynne Feifer: I love you like crazy, friend. And we will always agree on the Red Sox being the best, but we're going to have to continue to agree to disagree on the Patriots. HA! Go Bills!

To Ada Stutzman: Thank you for giving me YOUR bread and for being my friend.

Psalm 34:8: Taste and see that the Lord is good! Blessed is the man who trusteth in Him!

ABOUT THE AUTHOR

A lifelong lover of bread who only cuts carbs with a knife, Rebecca Lindamood is the author of *Not Your Mama's Canning Book* and the blog Foodie with Family. A respected voice in the food blogger community, she learned to bake at a young age by the side of her parents and grandmother and carried the love of baking fresh bread into her adult life. In addition to blogging full time, she is a part-time ballet and movement photographer. She is married to her biggest culinary fan and is mom to her five wild and crazy sons. Her free time is packed with enjoying Herculean amounts of iced tea (unsweetened, of course) and old-school mystery novels, and eating many, many scoops of ice cream.

INDEX